Engineering Science N. R. EVEROTT.

(Incorporating the Second Edition of Mechanical Engineering Science)

By the same authors

Applied Mechanics

Engineering Science

(Incorporating the Second Edition of
Mechanical Engineering Science)

D Titherington
B Eng (Liverpool), CEng, MIMechE, MInstMC

and

J G Rimmer
B Sc (Eng) (London), CEng, MIMechE
Wigan College of Technology

McGRAW-HILL Book Company (UK) Limited

London · New York · St Louis · San Francisco · Auckland
Bogotá · Guatemala · Hamburg · Johannesburg · Lisbon
Madrid · Mexico · Montreal · New Delhi · Panama · Paris
San Juan · São Paulo · Singapore · Sydney · Tokyo
Toronto

Published by
McGRAW-HILL Book Company (UK) Limited
MAIDENHEAD · BERKSHIRE · ENGLAND

British Library Cataloguing in Publication Data

Titherington, Derek
  Engineering science.
  1. Engineering
  I. Title   II. Rimmer, John Gordon
  III. Titherington, Derek. Mechanical engineering science
  620   TA145   79-41463

ISBN 0-07-084620-0

1234 B & S 83210

PRINTED AND BOUND IN GREAT BRITAIN

Contents

CONTENTS

Preface

With the advent of TEC Certificate and Diploma courses in engineering and the consequential phasing out of National Certificate and City and Guilds Technician courses, the need has arisen to revise or replace existing text books designed for Technician Engineers.

The authors' earlier work was written to suit the requirements of the first year National Certificate syllabus in Mechanical Engineering Science. That syllabus differed considerably from the TEC standard unit for Level II Engineering Science (U76/053) for which this book is intended. However, such was the popularity of the earlier book that those parts of its text which are relevant to the TEC unit have been retained in this new work. Furthermore, in the preparation of this new book, a similar style of presentation has been adopted in the hope that students and lecturers using it will find it equally satisfactory.

Apart from meeting the needs of TEC Standard Unit U76/053 in Engineering Science, the authors feel that, because of its content and logical order of presentation, this book will also prove to be of value to students taking any basic course in engineering.

Once again, the authors have enjoyed the friendly co-operation and helpful advice of an excellent publishing company. They would like to thank McGraw-Hill Book Company (UK) for this as well as for their patience. Thanks are also due to the various reviewers whose constructive criticisms have led to improvements in the final version of the text.

D Titherington
J G Rimmer

SI Units

Quantity	Name of unit	Unit symbol
Mass	kilogramme	kg
Length	metre	m
Time	second	s
Temperature	kelvin	K
Electric current	ampere	A
Luminous intensity	candela	cd

Names of multiples and submultiples

Factor by which the unit is to be multiplied	Prefix	Symbol
$1\,000\,000\,000\,000 = 10^{12}$	tera	T
$1\,000\,000\,000 = 10^{9}$	giga	G
$1\,000\,000 = 10^{6}$	mega	M
$1000 = 10^{3}$	kilo	k
$100 = 10^{2}$	hecto*	h
$10 = 10^{1}$	deca*	da
$0.1 = 10^{-1}$	deci*	d
$0.01 = 10^{-2}$	centi*	c
$0.001 = 10^{-3}$	milli	m
$0.000\,001 = 10^{-6}$	micro	μ
$0.000\,000\,001 = 10^{-9}$	nano	n
$0.000\,000\,000\,001 = 10^{-12}$	pico	p
$0.000\,000\,000\,000\,001 = 10^{-15}$	femto	f
$0.000\,000\,000\,000\,000\,001 = 10^{-18}$	atto	a

*Not recommended

Derived SI units having special names

Force

The newton (N) is that force which, applied to a body having a mass of 1 kg, gives it an acceleration of 1 m/s^2.

$$1\,N = 1\,kg\,m/s^2$$

Energy

The joule (J) is the work done when the point of application of a force of 1 N is displaced through a distance of 1 m in the direction of the force.

$$1\,J = 1\,N\,m$$

Power

The watt (W) is a rate of energy transfer of one joule per second.

$$1\,W = 1\,J/s$$

Frequency

The hertz (Hz) is the frequency of a periodic phenomenon of which the periodic time is 1 s.

$$1\,Hz = 1\,cycle/second$$

Acceptable non-SI units

Quantity	SI unit	Acceptable non-SI unit
mass	kg	tonne (t) = 10^3 kg or 1 Mg
time	s	day; hour (h); minute (min)
area	m^2	are (a) = 10^2 m^2
volume	m^3	litre (l) = 10^{-3} m^3
density	kg/m^3	t/m^3 = kg/l
pressure	N/m^2	bar (bar) = 10^5 N/m^2
velocity	m/s	km/h = (1/3.6) m/s
energy	J	kW h = 3.6 MJ

1. Dynamics

1.1 Vector quantities

In the fields of science and engineering, many different physical quantities are encountered. These quantities may be divided into two groups.

The first of these groups contains those physical quantities with which the concept of direction can never be associated. Such quantities are known as 'scalar' quantities. Examples of scalar quantities are mass, volume, energy, and time.

98.1 units

Figure 1.1

All the physical quantities in the second group possess *direction* as well as magnitude. These are called *vector quantites*. Examples of vector quantities are displacement, velocity, acceleration, force, and momentum. In order to define a vector quantity, it is necessary always to specify both the magnitude and the direction of the quantity. Furthermore, in addition to describing the direction of the quantity, an indication should be made of its *sense*. For example, the force due to gravity acting on a mass of 10 kg is defined thus:

magnitude: 98.1 newtons (see Section 1.9)
direction: vertical
sense: downwards

1

A fourth consideration may be important in certain types of problem: this is its position in space, or line of action, relative to some body.

Vector quantities can most conveniently be represented by means of *vectors*. A vector is a straight line drawn parallel to the direction of the quantity, and of a length proportional to the magnitude of the quantity. The sense may be indicated by an appropriate arrow on the vector. It is, however, important to understand that a vector does not represent the position of the quantity in space.

Figure 1.1 shows a vector representing the force due to gravity on the 10 kg mass referred to above.

1.2 Addition and subtraction of vectors

When two or more physical quantities of the same type are allowed to exert their influence on a particular situation, it is important to know the total, or resultant, effect on the situation. This is, in fact, the purpose of addition (or subtraction if negative quantities are involved). In the case of scalar quantities, numerical addition is all that is needed to achieve the total effect. With vector quantities, however, mere numerical addition is valid only if the quantities all happen to possess the same direction. In general, of course, the vector quantities will tend to have different directions and, in the addition process, the effect of these different directions must be taken into account.

Perhaps the simplest example of vector addition occurs when a body undergoes a series of displacements. With reference to Fig. 1.2, suppose a body is initally at o; is subsequently moved from o to

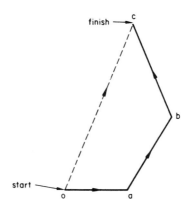

Figure 1.2

a; then from a to b; and finally from b to c. The net result is that the body has been displaced *from* o *to* c. This is expressed mathematically as follows:

$$\text{vector sum} = \mathbf{oa} + \mathbf{ab} + \mathbf{bc} = \mathbf{oc} \qquad (1.1)$$

The same rules of addition apply to all vector quantities, so that Eq. 1.1 and Fig. 1.2 represent the vector addition of any three vector quantities, whether they be displacements, velocities, accelerations, forces, etc.

Note that:

the sense of the vector sum is *from* the starting point *to* the finishing point;

the magnitude of $\mathbf{oc}$ is markedly different from the numerical sum of the magnitudes of $\mathbf{oa}$, $\mathbf{ab}$, and $\mathbf{bc}$;

small letters are always used to designate vectors;

the order in which the letters are quoted is indicative of the sense of the vector – thus, the resultant is $\mathbf{oc}$ and not $\mathbf{co}$, which would have the opposite sense.

Suppose now the difference between two vector quantities is required. In general, they will not have the same direction, so that the two quantities could be represented by the vectors $\mathbf{oa}$ and $\mathbf{ob}$, as shown in Fig. 1.3. Notice that in this case the vectors are drawn radiating from the same point o, whereas in the previous case the vectors were drawn end-to-end (Fig. 1.2).

$$\text{Vector difference } (\mathbf{oa} - \mathbf{ob}) = \mathbf{oa} + (-\mathbf{ob}) = \mathbf{oa} + \mathbf{bo}$$
$$= \mathbf{bo} + \mathbf{oa} = \mathbf{ba} \qquad (1.2)$$

By appreciating that a negative vector is one of opposite sense,

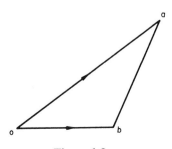

Figure 1.3

3

the vector difference has been converted into a vector sum in which b is the starting point and a is the finishing point.

In the same way, the vector difference $(\mathbf{ob} - \mathbf{oa})$ is given by

$$(\mathbf{ob} - \mathbf{oa}) = \mathbf{ob} + \mathbf{ao} = \mathbf{ao} + \mathbf{ob} = \mathbf{ab} \qquad (1.3)$$

which has, of course, the opposite sense.

1.3 Resolution of vectors

Figure 1.2 shows how a number of vector quantities may be combined to give their resultant effect. It is conversely true that a single vector quantity, as represented by **oc** (Fig. 1.2), may be replaced by the three vector quantities **oa**, **ab**, and **bc**, since their combined effect is the same. When this is done, the vector quantity is said to have been *resolved* into component parts. A single vector quantity can always be resolved, in this way, into *any* number of components in an infinite variety of different ways.

The resolution of a vector quantity into component parts can sometimes simplify the solution of an engineering problem. Usually, however, the most convenient resolution is one in which the vector quantity is resolved into two components at right angles.

For example, the vector **oa** in Fig. 1.4 could be resolved into the horizontal and vertical components **ox** and **xa**, respectively. By simple trigonometry,

$$\cos \theta = H/F; \qquad \sin \theta = V/F$$

Thus the horizontal component,

$$H = F \cos \theta \qquad (1.4)$$

and the vertical component,

$$V = F \sin \theta \qquad (1.5)$$

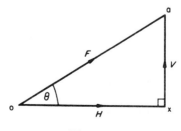

Figure 1.4

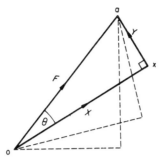

Figure 1.5

It should be noticed that the component *adjacent* to the angle θ is associated with the *cosine* of the angle; whereas the component *opposite* to the angle θ is associated with the *sine* of the angle.

Components at right angles need not, of course, be horizontal and vertical. Figure 1.5 shows another case in which a vector **oa** has been resolved into components at right angles, With reference to Fig. 1.5, and by comparison with Eqs 1.4 and 1.5,

$$X = F \cos \theta \qquad (1.6)$$

$$Y = F \sin \theta \qquad (1.7)$$

since X is the component adjacent to the angle θ, and Y is the component opposite to the angle θ.

There is, in fact, an infinite number of different ways in which a single vector may be resolved into two components at right angles.

An alternative method of illustrating the resolution of a vector quantity into two components at right angles is given in Fig. 1.6.

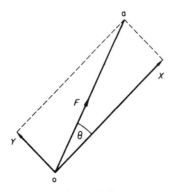

Figure 1.6

The right-angled triangle employed previously is here replaced by a rectangle, but comparison of Fig. 1.6 with Fig. 1.5 shows that the same result has been achieved. Both components, X and Y, are drawn radiating from the same point o. This method is convenient when the vector diagram is drawn superimposed on a space diagram, and o has some special significance in space. For example, o might be a simple pin-point connecting two elements of a mechanism or framework; or it might be the starting point of some body destined to undergo a displacement or be given some velocity.

1.4 Representation of velocities by vectors

As indicated in Section 1.1, velocity is a vector quantity and, as such, the direction of motion may be equally as important as the magnitude of the velocity. The magnitude of a velocity is often referred to as the 'speed', which term takes no account of direction. However, in most engineering problems direction of motion is of great importance so that the term 'velocity' – which does take account of direction – has much greater relevance.

Being a vector quantity, a velocity is most effectively represented by the drawing of a vector. An example of this shown in Fig. 1.7, in which a point A is depicted in the space diagram (a) as moving at the rate of 15 m/s in a direction making an angle θ with the horizontal. In the vector diagram (b), the velocity of A is represented by a line, 15 specified units of length long, drawn at the same angle. The sense of the velocity may be indicated by an arrow on the vector, but an indication of sense is also provided by defining the velocity as the vector **oa**, as opposed to **ao**. As will be appreciated by reading the next section, the velocity of A can be defined only in relation to some 'fixed' datum, for example the Earth, and, in this vector diagram, '**o**' represents this datum from which the velocity of A is measured. The small letters '**o**' and '**a**' are

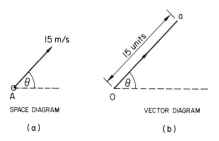

SPACE DIAGRAM   VECTOR DIAGRAM

(a)   (b)

Figure 1.7

described as the velocity images of the Earth and the point A, respectively.

In some cases, a point such as A may have two velocities at any given instant. For example, A could be a point in the engine mechanism of a moving vehicle, in which case it would have a velocity relative to the vehicle plus the velocity of the vehicle itself. The total, or resultant, velocity of A would then be given by the vector sum of these two velocities. In other cases, it may be necessary to evaluate the velocity of a point B relative to A, when A and B are both moving relative to the Earth. This is accomplished by vector subtraction as explained in the next section.

1.5 Relative velocity

By its very nature, all motion is relative. A body can only be said to 'move' if it changes its position in space relative to some other body. The whole concept of motion disappears when one supposes the existence of a single body in isolation. The displacement, velocity, and acceleration of a body may, therefore, be defined only in relation to some other body, or datum, which is usually regarded as 'fixed'.

It is most important to realize that the term 'fixed' is also a relative term. It is common practice, for example, to assume that the Earth is 'fixed', and velocities are accredited to bodies moving across its surface without any further reference being given. The Earth is by no means fixed, as everybody knows, but, for most purposes, it provides a very convenient datum from which to measure motion. In precisely the same way, other bodies, or points, may be used as reference data from which motion may be measured. These points may then also be described as 'fixed', or 'at rest', and this description is just as valid for these points as it is for the Earth.

To be correct, therefore, the reference datum should always be given when specifying a velocity. This includes the state of rest, which, after all, is only the particular case of zero velocity. Thus, the velocity of a point P may be measured *relative to a point A*, or *relative to a point B*, or *relative to the Earth*. The choice of datum is purely a matter of convenience.

The velocity of a point P, relative to a point A, is defined as the velocity with which P appears to be moving to an observer situated at and moving with A. For convenience, the following notation will be used:

$$\text{velocity of P relative to A} = v_{PA}$$
$$\text{velocity of P relative to B} = v_{PB}$$
$$\text{velocity of A relative to B} = v_{AB}, \text{ etc.}$$

7

The letter O is normally reserved for use as a symbol representing the Earth. When the reference datum is the Earth, however, the fact is frequently taken for granted. Thus, one might write:

$$\text{velocity of } P = v_P$$

whereas, more precisely, this should be written:

$$\text{velocity of P relative to the Earth} = v_{PO}$$

Consider two points, A and B, with velocities v_A and v_B (relative to the Earth), as shown in Fig, 1.8. In order to visualize the velocity of B relative to A, it is necessary to place oneself in the position of 'an observer situated at and moving with A'. To the occupant of a moving motor car, the dashboard, interior, and all other visible parts of the vehicle appear stationary, while the road, houses, and trees appear to be in motion. The only effective way, therefore, of becoming such an observer is to bring A to rest, without disturbing the relative motion of A and B. This may be achieved by imposing on *both* A and B (and on all other bodies, including the Earth), the velocity $-v_A$. Then,

$$\text{total velocity of A} = v_A - v_A = 0$$

$$\text{total velocity of B} = v_B - v_A = v_{BA}$$

$$\text{total velocity of the Earth} = 0 - v_A = -v_A$$

The point A is now 'fixed', and all other bodies are moving relative to it. Thus,

$$\text{velocity of B relative to A} = v_{BA} = v_B - v_A \qquad (1.8)$$

Note carefully that this is a *vector* difference. Figure 1.8 shows a possible method of combining the velocities v_B and $-v_A$ to give the resultant velocity v_{BA}, but reference should be made to Section 1.2 and Fig. 1.3, where a more general method of determining a vector difference is given. This method is used in the velocity vector diagram of Fig. 1.9, in which **oa** represents v_A, and **ob** represents v_B. The corresponding *small* letters **o**, **a**, and **b**, used in this vector diagram, are called *velocity images* of the Earth, point A, and point B, respectively. The velocity image of the Earth, **o**, has special

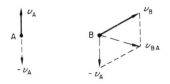

Figure 1.8

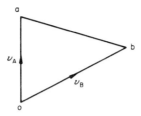

Figure 1.9

significance, and is known as the *pole* of the diagram. From Eq. 1.8,

velocity of B relative to $A = v_{BA} = v_B - v_A$

$$= \mathbf{ob} - \mathbf{oa}$$
$$= \mathbf{ob} + \mathbf{ao} \ (\text{since} -\mathbf{oa} = +\mathbf{ao})$$
$$= \mathbf{ao} + \mathbf{ob}$$
$$= \mathbf{ab}$$

Note that the vector representing the velocity of B, relative to A, starts at **a** and finishes at **b**, just as the vector representing the velocity of B, relative to the Earth, starts at **o** and finishes at **b**. Thus, the general rule to remember is that, for any velocity vector diagram:

a velocity *relative to A*, is measured *from* **a**;
a velocity *relative to B*, is measured *from* **b**;
a velocity *relative to the Earth*, is measured *from* **o**;

or, in other words, the velocity image of the stated reference datum is the point *from* which all velocities are measured. If this rule is remembered, and understood, there should be no difficulty in reading a velocity vector diagram correctly to give the magnitude, direction, and sense of any velocity.

Velocity diagrams, such that of Fig. 1.9, do not give any information regarding the relative *positions* of points in space. If such information is required, then a *space diagram*, or 'map' of the situation, is required. In many problems, both relative velocities and relative positions of bodies may be needed. For these problems, it is necessary to draw both a velocity diagram and a space diagram. In Fig. 1.10, the space diagram indicates the positions of two points, A and B, at a particular instant. A and B have velocities, relative to the Earth, as shown, and the velocity diagram gives their magnitudes, directions, and senses. If A is taken as the reference datum, i.e., assuming A is 'fixed', B will move with the velocity v_{BA} which is

1. DYNAMICS

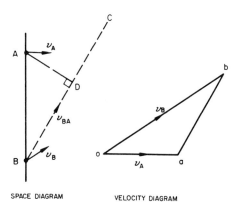

SPACE DIAGRAM   VELOCITY DIAGRAM

Figure 1.10

given by vector **ab**. Thus, if A is regarded as 'fixed', B will move along the path BC at speed v_{BA}. The shortest distance between A and B, at any time, will be AD, and the time taken for B to reach this position of closest approach is given by BD/v_{BA} (distance/velocity).

1.6 Linear velocity and acceleration

In Section 1.4, a distinction was made between the terms 'speed' and 'velocity'. Velocity can be defined as speed in a specified direction. If attention is confined to motion in a straight line, or *rectilinear* motion, this distinction loses its importance.

When a point moves, it changes its position in space. The measure of this change is the straight line connecting the initial and final positions of the point in space. This straight line is known as its *linear displacement, s.* Any such displacement takes time, and the displacement occurring in one unit of time, or rate of displacement, is called the *linear velocity* of the point.

For uniform motion in a straight line, the rate of displacement is constant and its measurement is quite straightforward. All that is necessary is to measure the time taken for a given displacement. For instance, if the displacement of a point over a distance of 20 m takes 5 s, the rate of displacement must be 4 m every second, or 4 m/s. This assumes that the rate of displacement does not vary over the 5 s period.

Thus, for uniform motion in a straight line,

$$\text{linear velocity} = v = \frac{\text{displacement}}{\text{time taken}} = \frac{s}{t} \qquad (1.9)$$

In general, the rate of displacement, i.e., velocity, will not remain constant during a displacement time period, and to determine its value at any particular instant in time is more difficult. What can be done is to measure the displacement from the starting position at regular time intervals, and plot a displacement/time graph, as shown in Fig. 1.11. Points A and B on this graph represent the displacements of a point at instants separated by a very short time interval. Over such a small time period, variation in velocity will be slight, so that Eq. 1.9 may be used to assess its velocity during this small time interval.

Thus,

$$\frac{\text{velocity over the}}{\text{short time interval}} = \frac{\text{change in displacement}}{\text{short time interval}} = \frac{BC}{AC}$$

$$= \text{slope of the chord AB}$$

If the short time interval is reduced still further, the slope of the chord AB will tend to become the slope of a tangent drawn at A. Therefore,

$$\text{velocity at A} = \frac{\text{Slope of the tangent at A}}{\text{on the displacement/time graph}} \qquad (1.10)$$

This definition gives the *instantaneous* value of the velocity, when the time period over which it is measured is regarded as infinitely small. The term *average velocity* relates to a measurement taken over a finite period of time, and is defined thus:

$$\frac{\text{average velocity}}{\text{over a finite time period}} = \frac{\text{total displacement}}{\text{total time period}} \qquad (1.11)$$

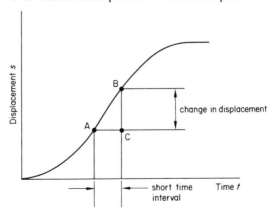

Figure 1.11

11

It should be appreciated that, throughout the period of time over which the total displacement is measured, the linear velocity, as given by Eq. 1.10, may vary continuously. The exception, of course, is the case of uniform motion, for which Eqs 1.9 and 1.11 are identical.

When the velocity of a point changes with time, it is said to possess an *acceleration*. An acceleration may be either positive or negative depending on whether the velocity is increasing or decreasing, respectively. A negative acceleration is often referred to as a 'deceleration', or as a 'retardation', and these terms imply that the velocity is reducing with time.

An acceleration is defined as the rate of change of velocity with time. Changes of velocity may be measured over a specified finite time period, and the average acceleration over this time period calculated by means of the following equation:

$$\text{average acceleration} = \frac{\text{total change in velocity}}{\text{total time period}} \quad (1.12)$$

Again, it must be appreciated that during this finite time period, the acceleration, or rate of change of velocity, may vary. At any given instant, the acceleration will have some instantaneous value, which can only be assessed by plotting a graph showing the variation of velocity with time, as illustrated in Fig. 1.12. With reference to Fig. 1.12, A and B represent the velocities of a point at the beginning and end of a very short time period during which any variation in acceleration may be considered slight. Thus,

$$\frac{\text{acceleration measured}}{\text{over the short time period}} = \frac{\text{change in velocity}}{\text{short time interval}} = \frac{BC}{AC}$$

$$= \text{slope of the chord AB}$$

Reducing the very short time interval to an infinitely small time period, this becomes

$$\text{acceleration at A} = \frac{\text{slope of the tangent at A}}{\text{on the velocity/time graph}} \quad (1.13)$$

This definition give the instantaneous value of the acceleration at the time corresponding to point A on the graph.

Velocity/time graphs are particularly useful because, in addition to providing information regarding velocities and accelerations at various times, it is also possible to obtain from them displacement

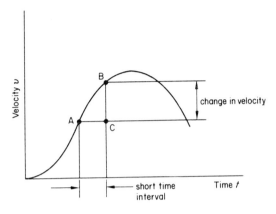

Figure 1.12

values. Since, in general,

$$\text{velocity} = \frac{\text{displacement}}{\text{time}}$$

it follows that

$$\text{displacement} = \text{velocity} \times \text{time}$$

Unit area on a velocity/time graph represents:

$$\text{unit velocity} \times \text{unit time}$$

as indicated in Fig. 1.13(a). It therefore follows that each unit of area on a velocity/time graph must represent a unit of displacement.

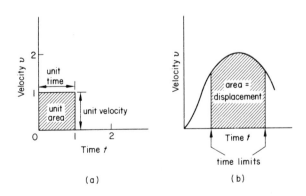

Figure 1.13

13

If this argument is developed further, it becomes clear that:

$$\begin{matrix} \text{Total area under} \\ \text{a velocity/time graph} \\ \text{between specified time limits} \end{matrix} = \begin{matrix} \text{Total displacement} \\ \text{during the period} \\ \text{between those time limits} \end{matrix} \qquad (1.14)$$

as indicated in Fig. 1.13(b).

Summarizing, it may be said that problems involving the motion in a straight line of a point or body may be solved by drawing, or sketching, a velocity/time graph. From this graph, the following information may be deduced:

(a) *velocities* at specified times by reading off the *scales* directly;
(b) *accelerations* at specified times by measuring the *slopes* of the tangents at points corresponding to these times;
(c) *displacement* over a specified time period by measuring the *area* under the graph between appropriate time limits.

Motion with uniform acceleration

Many instances occur in practice in which a point or body moves with a constant or uniform acceleration. This is, therefore, an important special case. From Eq. 1.13, it follows that if the acceleration is constant, the slope of the velocity/time graph will not vary, i.e., it will be a straight line graph. Figure 1.14 shows a velocity/time, or speed/time, graph describing the motion of a body having constant acceleration.

For the case shown, the body has an initial speed u, which increases to speed v during a period of time t. The distance travelled, s, is represented by the area of the diagram (which is a

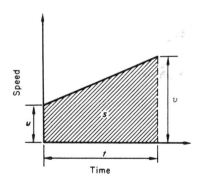

Figure 1.14

trapezium) and the acceleration a is given by the slope of the graph.

$$s = \text{area of trapezium} = \tfrac{1}{2}(u + v)\, t \qquad (1.15)$$

$$a = \text{slope of graph} = (v - u)/t \qquad (1.16)$$

Note that, for constant acceleration, the average speed, which is equal to the mean height of the diagram, is $\tfrac{1}{2}(u + v)$. This is *only* true for the particular case of uniform acceleration. Equation 1.15 thus reads: total distance = average speed × time, which is only a restatement of Eq. 1.11. In the same way, Eq. 1.16 may be expressed in words:

acceleration = increase in speed/time taken

which is in accordance with the basic concept of acceleration.

These equations are a pair of simultaneous equations involving five variables, only four of which appear in any one equation. By eliminating each of the variables in turn, three further equations may be deduced. These are: $s = ut + \tfrac{1}{2}at^2$; $v^2 = u^2 + 2as$; $s = vt - \tfrac{1}{2}at^2$. Since in almost every case the initial speed u is known, there is little point in eliminating it from the equation. For this reason, the last equation is of little importance and may be discarded.

To sum up, although there are only two basic equations (1.15 and 1.16), two further equations may be deduced to provide four useful relationships for the solution of problems involving uniform acceleration:

$$\left.\begin{aligned} s &= \tfrac{1}{2}(u + v)t \\ v &= u + at \\ s &= ut + \tfrac{1}{2}at^2 \\ v^2 &= u^2 + 2as \end{aligned}\right\} \qquad (1.17)$$

On no account must Eqs 1.17 be used where a change of acceleration occurs during the time period t.

1.7 Newton's laws of motion

When a body has motion, there are two questions which an engineer must ask. What is the velocity of the body? How much matter is moving with this velocity? The answers to these questions are represented, respectively, by the velocity, v, and the mass, m, of the body. If either is increased, then so is the total 'quantity of motion' of the system. It follows that the product of mass and velocity is a measure of the 'quantity of motion' of the body, and this is called the *momentum* of the body,

$$\text{momentum of the body} = mv \qquad (1.18)$$

It should be clear from this definition that a small mass with a large velocity may have the same momentum, or quantity of motion, as a large mass with a small velocity. Since velocity is a vector quantity, the product of mass and velocity must also be a vector quantity. Thus, momentum is a vector quantity, and consideration must always be given to its direction and sense, as well as its magnitude.

Although most people are familiar with the concept of force, it is a quantity not easy to define. It may be said that force is that which tends to alter the relative motion of, or to change the shape of, the body to which it is applied. A force can be recognized only by its effect on the body to which it is applied. A force must therefore be measured in terms of these effects.

The laws governing the effect of a force on the motion of a body have been set out by Sir Isaac Newton.

1. *A body continues in its present state of rest or uniform motion in a straight line unless acted upon by some external force.*
2. *The rate of change of momentum of a body is directly proportional to the resultant external force which is producing the change.*
3. *To every action there is an equal and opposite reaction.*

Newton's first law is a simple statement of the fact that if a force is applied to a body, the body will be affected in some way. If the force is unresisted, then the only effect possible is a change in its state of motion. The tendency of a body to continue in its present state of motion is called its *inertia*, and this property is found to be dependent on the mass of the body. The state of motion of the body is defined by its velocity, which is a vector quantity and may be changed in either magnitude or direction, or both. In considering the effect of a force on a body, therefore, the two quantities 'mass' and 'velocity' are very important, and these are embodied in the concept of momentum.

Newton's second law postulates a relationship between the applied force and the change of momentum produced in a given time. This is a reasonable proposition, but one which requires verification by experiment.

Newton's third law is concerned with the resulting effects on the agency providing the external force. For example, a moving railway truck may be brought to rest by a pair of spring-loaded buffers. The buffers exert a force on the truck, thereby changing its momentum. This force may be detected and measured by observing its effect on the truck. However, it is also clear that the truck exerts a force on the buffers, as is evidenced by the compression of the buffer springs. These forces are equal and opposite.

1.8 Newton's second law of motion

This law is perhaps the most important of the three, since it provides a means of *measuring* a force.

Consider a body of mass m which is moving with a velocity u. Let an unresisted force F be applied to the body, so that a change of momentum will take place. Suppose that, after a time t, the body has a velocity v,

initial momentum of the body $= mu$

final momentum of the body $= mv$

$\qquad$ change in momentum $=$ final momentum $-$ initial momentum

$$= mv - mu$$

(Note that this a vector difference.)

$$\text{Rate of change of momentum} = \frac{\text{change in momentum}}{\text{time taken}}$$

$$= \frac{mv - mu}{t}$$

Then, according to Newton's second law,

$$F \propto \frac{mv - mu}{t}$$

If the mass, m, of the body remains constant, this may be written:

$$F \propto m \frac{(v - u)}{t}$$

But, from Eq. 1.16

$$\frac{(v - u)}{t} = a$$

where a is the acceleration of the body, so that:

$$F \propto ma \qquad\qquad (1.19)$$

Equation 1.19 shows that the effect of a *force* on a body of constant mass, m, is to give it an *acceleration* in the same direction as the force. Furthermore, the equation also shows that force must have the dimensions of mass $\times$ acceleration,

$$\text{dimensions of force} = M\left(\frac{L}{T^2}\right) = MLT^{-2}$$

The unit of force may now be defined as the force required to give unit mass unit acceleration. In SI units, the unit of mass is the kilogramme (kg), and the unit of acceleration is the metre per second per second (m/s^2). The corresponding unit of force is called the *newton* (N).

1 newton is defined as *the force required to give a mass of 1 kg an acceleration of* 1 *m/s*^{2}. That is:

$$1\ N = 1\ kg\ m/s^2$$

With this system of units specified, the equation derived from Newton's second law may now be written:

$$F = ma \qquad (1.20)$$

1.9 The gravitational force on a body

The force of attraction between the Earth and a body is known as the force due to gravity. This force is proportional to the mass of the body, and it follows that the acceleration due to gravity will be the same for all masses.

From Newton's second law,

$$a = \frac{F}{m} = \frac{\text{constant} \times m}{m} = \text{constant}$$

This constant acceleration is normally denoted by the symbol g, and has the value of 9.81 m/s^2,

$$\text{acceleration due to gravity} = g = 9.81\ m/s^2 \qquad (1.21)$$

Newton's second law may now be used to express the force due to gravity which acts on a body:

gravitational force on a body = mass × gravitational acceleration

That is,

$$\text{gravitational force} = mg \qquad (1.22)$$

Thus, the force due to gravity on a mass of 10 kg will be 98.1 N.

1.10 Angular velocity and acceleration

When a body undergoes angular motion, its position in space may remain unaltered. Its orientation in space will, however, change, and the measure of this change is its *angular displacement*, which is the angle through which it turns relative to some datum. This is normally denoted by the symbol θ, and the unit of measurement is the radian (see Section 1.11). Angular displacement is a vector quantity, its direction being indicated by the axis of rotation and its sense being described as either clockwise or anticlockwise. Problems involving changes in the axis of rotation will not, however, be encountered at the level for which this text is intended, so that only the magnitude and sense of an angular displacement need be considered here.

As for the case of linear motion (Section 1.6), an angular displacement takes time in which to occur, and the rate of angular displacement, or angular velocity, is given by the equation:

$$\text{angular velocity} = \omega = \frac{\text{angular displacement}}{\text{time taken}} = \frac{\theta}{t} \qquad (1.23)$$

This simple equation refers only to rotations which take place at constant speed. Angular velocities can vary and, as for linear motion, an instantaneous value of an angular velocity can be assessed only by measuring the slope of an angular displacement/time graph. Thus, in general,

$$\text{angular velocity, } \omega = \text{slope of angular displacement/time graph} \qquad (1.24)$$

For a non-uniform angular velocity, an average value can be calculated using the equation:

$$\text{average angular velocity} = \frac{\text{total angular displacement}}{\text{total time taken}} \qquad (1.25)$$

The angular acceleration, α, of a rotating body is defined as the rate of change of angular velocity. Thus,

$$\text{angular acceleration} = \alpha = \frac{\text{change in angular velocity}}{\text{time taken}} \qquad (1.26)$$

Again, this equation refers only to the case in which the angular velocity changes at a constant rate. More generally,

$$\text{angular acceleration, } \alpha = \text{slope of angular velocity/time graph} \qquad (1.27)$$

The argument in justification of this equation is the same as that relating to linear acceleration (Eq. 1.13). Furthermore, it can also be stated that the area under an angular velocity/time graph represents angular displacement, again, by virtue of the same reasoning used in Section 1.6.

In short, an angular velocity/time graph is just as useful in solving problems involving angular motion, as the linear velocity/time graph

19

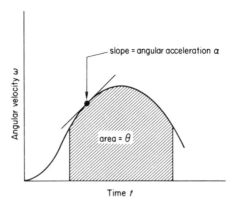

Figure 1.15

is for linear motion problems. Its area represents angular displacement, and its slope represents angular acceleration, as indicated in Fig. 1.15.

For *constant angular acceleration*, the angular velocity/time graph will be a straight line, and equations similar to those of Eqs 1.17 relating to linear motion may be developed for angular motion. These are:

$$\left.\begin{aligned}
\theta &= \frac{(\omega_1 + \omega_2)}{2}\, t \\
\omega_2 &= \omega_1 + \alpha t \\
\theta &= \omega_1 t + \frac{1}{2}\,\alpha t^2 \\
\omega_2^2 &= \omega_1^2 + 2\alpha\theta
\end{aligned}\right\} \qquad (1.28)$$

1.11 Relation between linear and angular motion

The distance travelled by a point which moves along a circular path, such as AB in Fig. 1.16(b), is clearly related to the radius of the circle, r, and the angle θ subtended by the arc AB at its centre. In order to express this relationship simply, a unit of angular measure, called the 'radian', is defined.

One radian is the angle subtended at the centre of a circle by an arc whose length is equal to the radius of the circle. An angle of 1 radian is illustrated in Fig. 1.16(a).

With reference to Fig. 1.16(b), the number of radians subtended at the centre O by the arc AB, whose length is s, may be obtained

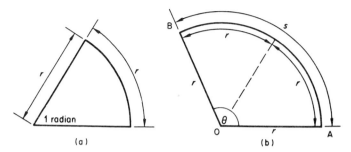

Figure 1.16

by discovering how many lengths equal to the radius r are equivalent to the length s. For the case shown, the answer is obviously 2, but in general:

$$\theta = (s/r)\ \text{rad} \tag{1.29}$$

Conversely, *provided θ is measured in radians*, the distance travelled along a circular arc of radius r may be calculated from Eq. 1.29. Transposing, this becomes

$$s = r\theta \tag{1.30}$$

Since the complete circumference of a circle subtends an angle of $360°$ at its centre and the length of the circumference is $2\pi r$, the conversion factor relating degrees and radians is given by:

$$360° = (2\pi r/r)\ \text{rad}$$
$$360° = 2\pi\ \text{rad} \tag{1.31}$$

The time taken for a point to travel along a circular arc, of length s, is of necessity the same as the time taken by the corresponding radial arm to rotate through the angle θ. If this time is t, then, from Eq. 1.30,

$$(s/t) = r(\theta/t)$$

average linear speed $= r \times$ average angular speed

If θ is now made very small, the average linear speed, over the correspondingly very small time, becomes the instantaneous linear velocity, v, and the average angular speed becomes the instantaneous angular velocity, ω. Thus,

$$v = r\omega \tag{1.32}$$

where v is the instantaneous value of the linear velocity, and ω is the instantaneous value of the angular velocity, *measured in radian/second*, and r is the radius of curvature of the path.

1. DYNAMICS

In a similar manner, an equation relating linear and angular acceleration may be deduced from Eq. 1.32. This equation is:

$$a = r\alpha \qquad (1.33)$$

In mechanical engineering science, the relationships expressed by Eqs 1.30, 1.32, and 1.33 are constantly in use. For this reason, it is essential that they be memorized.

Worked examples

1. Draw vectors to represent the following physical quantities:

   (a) a force of 7.5 kN acting in an upward direction 30° to the horizontal;
   (b) a horizontal velocity of 20 m/s.

   (a) The vector representing the force of 7.5 kN is shown in Fig. 1.17(a)
   The scale is 10 mm = 1 kN.
   (b) The vector representing the velocity of 20 m/s is shown in Fig. 1.17(b).
   The scale is 10 mm = 4 m/s.

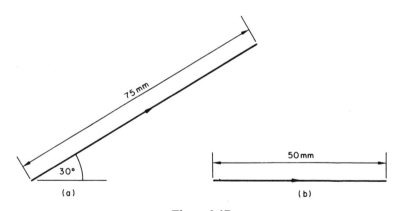

Figure 1.17

2. A fork-lift truck is capable of raising a load at the rate of 0.5 m/s. The guides of the lifting mechanism are inclined backwards at 5° to the vertical to prevent the load slipping off the forks. Determine the resultant velocity of the load if, while lifting the load at this rate, the truck moves forward at 1.5 m/s.

22

The resultant velocity will be the vector sum of the two given velocities.

With reference to Fig. 1.18, the resultant velocity = **oa** + **ab** = **ob** = 1.54 m/s at 18° 53' to the horizontal.

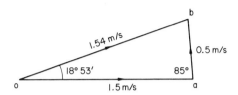

Figure 1.18

3. Determine the vector difference between two velocities of 15 m/s and 8 m/s, the angle between their directions being 30°.

The sense of the vector difference is not specified, so that, with reference to Fig. 1.19,

$$\text{vector difference} = (\mathbf{oa} - \mathbf{ob}) \quad \text{or} \quad (\mathbf{ob} - \mathbf{oa})$$
$$= (\mathbf{bo} + \mathbf{oa}) \quad \text{or} \quad (\mathbf{ao} + \mathbf{ob})$$
$$= \mathbf{ba} \text{ or } \mathbf{ab}$$

= 9.0 m/s, in a direction making an angle of 26° 23' with the velocity of 15 m/s

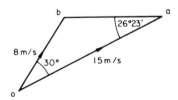

Figure 1.19

4. A force of 150 kN is applied to one end of a straight member and at 20° to its axis. The other end of the member is fixed. Calculate the axial and transverse components of the force.

The space and vector diagrams are shown in Fig. 1.20.

The axial component = 150 cos 20° = 141.0 kN

The transverse component = 150 sin 20° = 51.3 kN

23

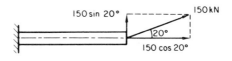

Figure 1.20

5. A projectile is given an initial velocity of 500 m/s in a direction 50° to the horizontal. The projectile is directed up a plane inclined at 7° to the horizontal. Calculate the components of the velocity parallel to and perpendicular to the incline.

The angle between the velocity and the inclined plane = 50° − 7° = 43°.

Component of velocity parallel to the plane = 500 cos 43°

= 365.7 m/s

Component of velocity perpendicular to the plane = 500 sin 43°

= 341.0 m/s

6. A counter recording the revolutions of a flywheel was read at 30 s intervals over a 4.5 min period, and the figures recorded were as follows:

0, 603, 2340, 5000, 8264, 11 736, 15 000, 17 660, 19 397, 20 000

Draw the space–time graph for the motion, and hence estimate the greatest and least speeds of rotation of the flywheel, and the times at which they occur.

What is the average speed of the flywheel over the 4.5 min period?

The space–time diagram is shown plotted in Fig. 1.21. From Eq. 1.24, the speed at any instant is given by the slope of this graph. By inspection, the greatest slope occurs half-way through the time period, i.e., at 2.25 min, when:

greatest speed = maximum slope = 17 500/2.5 = 7000 rev/min

The least slope is seen to be zero, at the beginning, and at the end of the time period, i.e., least speed = 0, at zero time and at 4.5 min.

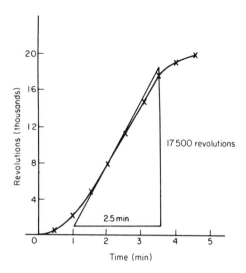

Figure 1.21

average speed of flywheel = total revs/total time = $20\,000/4.5$

$$= 4444 \text{ rev/min}$$

7. A motor car is driven along a road and its speed is recorded at 30 s intervals. The speedometer readings, in km/h, are:

$$0, \quad 18, \quad 28, \quad 36, \quad 42, \quad 45, \quad 46, \quad 42, \quad 27, \quad 15, \quad 0$$

Plot the speed–time diagram, and hence estimate: (a) the maximum acceleration and deceleration of the car; (b) the total distance travelled; (c) the average speed of the car.

The speedometer readings are first converted into m/s:

$$0, \quad 5, \quad 7.8, \quad 10, \quad 11.67, \quad 12.5, \quad 12.78, \quad 11.67, \quad 7.5, \quad 4.17, \quad 0$$

The speed–time graph is shown plotted in Fig. 1.22.

(a) The acceleration is given by the slope of this graph. By inspection, this is estimated to be a maximum at the start of the journey, i.e., $t = 0$,

$$\text{maximum acceleration} = 8.5/30 = 0.283 \text{ m/s}^2$$

The maximum deceleration, or maximum negative slope, is estimated to occur at $t = 230$ s, and also at the end of the journey, $t = 300$ s,

$$\text{maximum deceleration} = 10.5/60 = 0.175 \text{ m/s}^2$$

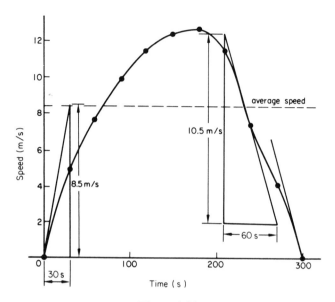

Figure 1.22

(b) Total distance travelled = total area under speed–time graph
   = 2530 m = 2.53 km

This area may be obtained by planimeter, mid-ordinate rule, or by any other accepted method.

(c) The average speed = total distance travelled/total time period
   = total area/base
   = mean height of the diagram
   = 2530/300 = 8.43 m/s or 30.36 km/h

8. A body accelerates uniformly from rest with a constant acceleration of 0.5 m/s² for a period of 8 s, and then continues to move at a constant speed.

Sketch the speed–time graph, and hence determine the time taken for the body to travel 25 m from the rest position.

The speed–time diagram is shown in Fig. 1.23.

Let V = the maximum speed. Then, since the acceleration is given by the slope of this graph,

$$\text{acceleration} = 0.5 = V/8$$

$$V = 8 \times 0.5 = 4 \text{ m/s}$$

Let t = the time taken for the body to travel 25 m from the rest

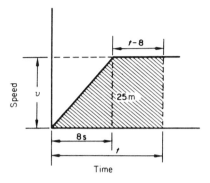

Figure 1.23

position,

$$\text{shaded area of the diagram} = 25 \text{ m} = \tfrac{1}{2}(t + t - 8)4$$
$$25 = (t - 4)4$$
$$t = 4 + 6.25 = 10.25 \text{ s}$$

9. The armature of an electric motor normally rotates at 8000 rev/min. When the motor is switched on, a time period of 12 s elapses before the normal running speed is reached.

Assuming constant acceleration, calculate (a) the angular acceleration and (b) the number of revolutions made by the armature during this time period.

$$\omega_1 = 0$$
$$\omega_2 = 8000 \times 2\pi/60 = 838 \text{ rad/s}$$
$$t = 12 \text{ s}$$
$$\alpha = ?$$
$$\theta = ?$$

(a) $\omega_2 = \omega_1 + \alpha t$
$$838 = 0 + \alpha 12$$
$$\alpha = 69.1 \text{ rad/s}^2$$

(b) $\theta = \tfrac{1}{2}(\omega_1 + \omega_2)t$
$$\theta = \tfrac{1}{2}(0 + 838)12$$
$$= 5028 \text{ rad}$$
$$n = 800 \text{ rev}$$

10. A body is projected vertically upwards with a velocity of 20 m/s. The point of projection is on the edge of a deep hole, so that, on returning to Earth, the body continues its descent to the bottom of the hole. The hole is 30 m deep. Assuming $g = 10 \text{ m/s}^2$, determine: (a) the maximum height reached; (b) the time taken to reach the maximum height; (c) the total time of flight; (d) the velocity with which the body strikes the bottom of the hole.

Consider the upward motion of the body:

$$
\left.
\begin{array}{l}
s = h \\
u = 20 \text{ m/s} \\
v = 0 \\
a = -g \\
t = ?
\end{array}
\right\}
\quad
\begin{array}{l}
v^2 = u^2 + 2as \\
0 = (20)^2 - 2gh \\
h = 400/(2 \times 10) \\
 = 20 \text{ m}
\end{array}
\quad
\begin{array}{l}
v = u + at \\
0 = 20 - gt \\
t = 20/10 \\
 = 2 \text{ s}
\end{array}
$$

(a) Maximum height reached above point of projection = 20 m.
(b) Time taken to reach maximum height = 2 s.
  Consider the whole of the motion:

$$
\left\{
\begin{array}{l}
\quad\quad s = ut + \tfrac{1}{2}at^2 \\
\quad\quad -30 = 20t - \tfrac{1}{2}gt^2 \\
\quad\quad 5t^2 - 20t - 30 = 0 \\
\quad\quad\quad t^2 - 4t - 6 = 0 \\
\\
\quad\quad t = \dfrac{4 \pm \sqrt{(16+24)}}{2} \\
\\
\quad\quad t = 2 + \sqrt{10}, \text{ or } 2 - \sqrt{10} \\
\quad\quad t = 2 + 3.162 = 5.162 \text{ s} \\
\text{(since the negative answer is impossible)} \\
\\
\quad\quad v = u + at \\
\quad\quad v = 20 - gt = 20 - (10 \times 5.162) \\
\quad\quad\quad = 20 - 51.62 = -31.62 \text{ m/s}
\end{array}
\right.
$$

$$
\begin{array}{l}
s = -30 \text{ m} \\
u = +20 \text{ m/s} \\
a = -g \\
v = ? \\
t = ?
\end{array}
$$

(c) Total time of flight = 5.162 s
(d) Velocity on reaching bottom of hole = 31.62 m/s (downwards)

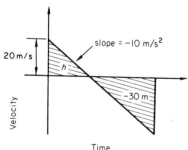

Figure 1.24

WORKED EXAMPLES

The velocity–time diagram for this motion is given in Fig. 1.24 from which the above answers may be deduced from simple geometry.

11. Two motor cars, A and B, are travelling along straight roads towards cross-roads C. The angle ACB is 60°. At a particular instant, which, for convenience, will be called zero time, car A is 5 km from C and is travelling at 100 km/h, while car B is 2 km from C and is travelling at 50 km/h.

Determine the shortest distance between the cars at any time, and the time at which this situation occurs.

The space and velocity diagrams are shown in Fig. 1.25. Let B be regarded as 'fixed'. Then:

velocity of A (relative to B) = **ba** = 86.6 km/h;
relative to B, A will move along the path AC', shown dotted in the space diagram, at the rate of 86.6 km/h;
shortest distance between the cars = BC' = 0.5 km;
time taken for A to move to C' = AC'/**ba**

$$= \frac{4.33 \text{ km}}{86.6 \text{ km/h}} = 0.05 \text{ h} = 3 \text{ min}$$

Note that in this same time, the point C has moved, relative to B, with the velocity **bc** to the position C'.

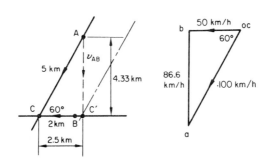

Figure 1.25

12. A body is lowered at a constant velocity of 2 m/s by means of a rope wound round a drum, as shown in Fig. 1.26 The effective diameter of the drum is 0.2 m.

Calculate the angular velocity of the drum in rev/min, and the number of revolutions it makes while the body descends 15 m.

29

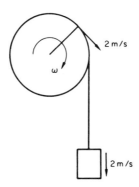

Figure 1.26

Assuming the rope does not stretch, each point on the rope has the same linear speed as the body. Thus, at any instant, linear velocity of a point on the circumference of the drum = 2 m/s. From Eq. 1.32,

angular velocity of the drum = $\omega = v/r = 2/0.1 = 20$ rad/s

If n is the speed of rotation in rev/min,

$$n = 20 \times 60/2\pi$$
$$= 191 \text{ rev/min}$$

As the body descends 15 m, this amount of rope is uncoiled from the drum.

From Eq. 1.29,

angle through which drum turns $= \theta = s/r$
$$= 15/0.1$$
$$= 150 \text{ rad}$$

number of revolutions made $= 150/2\pi = 23.9$ rev

13. Calculate the force required to give a truck of mass 1000 kg (1 tonne) an acceleration of 2 m/s².

From Newton's second law,

force = mass × acceleration
$$= 1000 \text{ kg} \times 2 \text{ m/s}^2$$
$$= 2000 \text{ kg m/s}^2$$
$$= 2000 \text{ N} = 2 \text{ kN}$$

14. Calculate the acceleration given to a body of mass 50 kg by a force of 1 kN applied vertically upwards.

A diagram should first be drawn, as in Fig. 1.27, showing *all* the forces acting on the body.

1000 N

50 kg

mg
(= 490.5 N)

Figure 1.27

In this case, there are two forces acting on the body:
the vertical upward force of 1000 N;
the force due to gravity which acts vertically downwards.
Force due to gravity $= mg = 50(9.81) = 490.5$ N.
From Fig. 1.27, *resultant* force on the body $= 1000 - 490.5 = 509.5$ N vertically upwards.
From Newton's second law,

$$F = ma$$

where F is the *resultant* force acting on the body.
Thus,

$$509.5 = 50a$$

$$a = \frac{509.5}{50} = 10.19 \text{ m/s}^2, \text{ vertically upwards.}$$

15. A body lying on a smooth horizontal surface is subjected to the action of three horizontal forces whose magnitudes and directions are shown in Fig. 1.28(a). If the acceleration of the body along the horizontal surface has a magnitude of 2 m/s², determine the direction of the acceleration and the mass of the body.

The resultant of the three forces must first be found by vector addition. From the force vector diagram of Fig. 1.28(b),

resultant force $= F = 51.4$ N, acting at 67° 6′, to the 10 N force

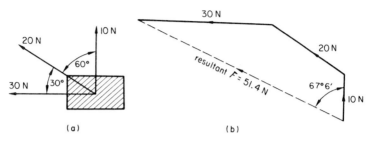

Figure 1.28

Since the acceleration must always be in the same direction as the resultant force, this is also the direction of the acceleration.
From Newton's second law,

$$F = ma$$
$$51.4 = m(2)$$
$$m = 51.4/2 = 25.7 \text{ kg}$$

16. Two masses of 10 kg and 20 kg lie on smooth planes inclined at 60° and 30° to the horizontal, respectively, and are connected by a light, inextensible string which passes over a smooth cylinder at the top of the planes, as shown in Fig. 1.29. Determine the acceleration of the system, and the tension in the string.

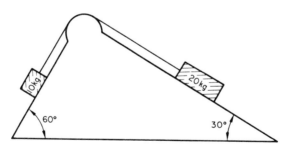

Figure 1.29

Where a number of bodies are involved in a problem, each body should be considered separately.

A diagram should be drawn for each body, showing *all* the forces acting on it, and an equation of motion for the body deduced from Newton's second law.

Let F_T be the tension in the string, and a the acceleration of the system. It will be assumed that the 10 kg mass accelerates *up* its plane, and the 20 kg mass accelerates *down* its plane. Should this assumption be incorrect, a negative answer will be obtained for *a*. Consider the 10 kg mass (Fig. 1.30). Three forces act on this mass: the force due to the tension in the string, acting up the plane; the force due to gravity, *mg*, acting vertically downwards; a normal reaction, R_1, exerted by the plane on the mass.

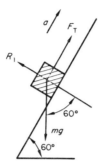

Figure 1.30

Since there can be no motion perpendicular to the plane, the effect of R_1 must be cancelled out by the component perpendicular to the plane of the force due to gravity. That is, resolving perpendicular to the plane, $R_1 = mg \cos 60°$.

The other component of the gravitational force, *mg* sin 60°, acts parallel to the plane and opposes the force F_T, which is pulling the mass up the plane.

Resultant force in the direction of motion $= F_T - mg \sin 60°$.

From Newton's second law,

$$F_T - mg \sin 60° = ma$$
$$F_T - 10g \sin 60° = 10a \qquad (1)$$

This is the equation of motion for the 10 kg mass.

Consider the 20 kg mass (Fig. 1.31).

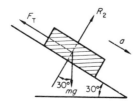

Figure 1.31

DYNAMICS

Again, since there can be no motion perpendicular to the plane:

$$R_2 = mg \cos 30°$$

Resultant force in the direction of motion $= mg \sin 30° - F_T$.
Note that, in this case, it is the tension F_T which opposes the gravitational force component pulling the mass down the plane.
From Newton's second law,

$$mg \sin 30° - F_T = ma$$
$$20g \sin 30° - F_T = 20a \qquad (2)$$

This is the equation of motion for the 20 kg mass.
Addition of Eqs. 1 and 2 gives:

$$20g \sin 30° - 10g \sin 60° = 20a + 10a$$

from which:

$$a = 1.34g/30 = 0.0447g = 0.438 \text{ m/s}^2$$

Substitution in Eq. 1 gives:

$$F_T - 10g \sin 60° = 10(0.438)$$
$$F_T = 8.66g + 4.38 = 89.33 \text{ N}$$

17. A lorry and trailer, initially at rest, accelerate uniformly along a level road, and after travelling 1 km reach a speed of 54 km/h. The mass of the lorry is 3 tonnes, and that of the trailer 2 tonnes. Frictional resistances are equivalent to 0.2 N/kg. Calculate the tractive effort required, and the draw-bar pull during the motion. (1 tonne = 1000 kg.)

The velocity–time diagram is shown in Fig. 1.32.

$$54 \text{ km/h} = 54\,000/3600 = 15 \text{ m/s}$$

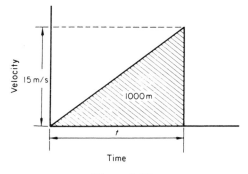

Figure 1.32

34

From this diagram,

$$\tfrac{1}{2}(t)\,15 = 1000 \text{ m}$$
$$t = 2000/15 = 133.3 \text{ s}$$
$$\text{acceleration} = 15/133.3 = 0.1125 \text{ m/s}^2$$

Consider the trailer (Fig. 1.33).

Let the draw-bar pull $= F_D$

frictional resistance $= 0.2(2000) = 400$ N

resultant force, $F = (F_D - 400)$ N

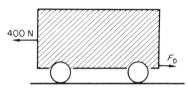

Figure 1.33

From Newton's second law,

$$F = ma$$
$$F_D - 400 = 2000(0.1125)$$
$$\text{draw-bar} = F_D = 400 + 225 = 625 \text{ N}$$

Consider the lorry (Fig. 1.34).

Let tractive effort $= F_E$

frictional resistance $= 0.2(3000) = 600$ N

resultant force, $F = (F_E - F_D - 600)$ N

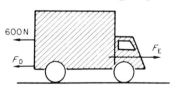

Figure 1.34

From Newton's second law,

$$F = ma$$
$$F_E - F_D - 600 = 3000(0.1125)$$
$$\text{tractive effort} = F_E = F_D + 600 + 337.5$$
$$= 625 + 600 + 337.5 = 1562.5 \text{ N}$$

Problems

1. Explain the difference between scalar and vector quantities, and quote five examples of each.

2. Choose suitable scales and draw vectors to represent the following physical quantities:

(a) an acceleration of 5 m/s^2 in a direction 25° to the horizontal and with an upward sense;
(b) a horizontal momentum of 85 kg m/s;
(c) a velocity of 65 km/h in a direction 20° west of north.

3. Four forces, F_1, F_2, F_3, F_4, act outwards from the same point. Their magnitudes are, respectively, 2.5 kN, 4.0 kN, 1.2 kN, and 6.0 kN. The forces, F_2, F_3, and F_4, are in directions making angles of 70°, 200°, and 280°, respectively, with F_1, all these angles being measured in the same sense.

Determine the vector sum of the forces.

(*Answer.* 4.57 kN at 325° 54′ to F_1.)

4. The velocity of a body changes from 5 m/s vertically upwards to 4 m/s in a horizontal direction. Determine the magnitude, direction, and sense of the change by substracting the initial velocity from the final velocity.

(*Answer.* 6.4 m/s, 38° 39′ to the vertical, downwards.)

5. The force on a piston is known to be 4.4 kN when the connecting rod makes an angle of 15° to the line of stroke.

Determine the axial and transverse components of this force relative to the connecting rod.

(*Answer.* 4.25 kN, 1.14 kN.)

6. In order to drill a hole in the correct position, it is necessary to move the drilling head a distance of 50 mm in a direction 35° to one edge of a rectangular plate.

Calculate the components of this displacement parallel and perpendicular to this edge.

(*Answer.* 40.96 mm, 26.68 mm.)

7. The displacement of a body from a given point is recorded at 20 s intervals. Beginning with that corresponding to zero time, the displacements, in metres, are:

0, 4, 16, 36, 64, 100, 130, 140, 130, 110, 90

From these figures, deduce: (a) the maximum speed of the body; (b) the time at which it occurs; (c) the times at which the velocity is zero; (d) the average velocity over the whole period; (e) the velocity at the end of this period.

(*Answer.* (a) 2 m/s (b) 100 s (c) 0 and 140 s (d) 0.45 m/s
(e) −1 m/s.)

8. The wheels of a motor car have an effective diameter of 0.6 m. The speed of the vehicle, in m/s, was noted at intervals of 1 min during a journey lasting 12 min. The figures recorded were as follows:

0, 1.2, 4.8, 9.0, 12.0, 13.8, 14.4, 13.8, 12.0, 9.0, 4.8, 1.2, 0

From these figures, estimate: (a) the total distance travelled by the vehicle; (b) the average speed of the vehicle; (c) the number of revolutions made by each of its wheels; (d) the maximum angular velocity of each wheel; (e) the maximum acceleration and deceleration of the vehicle, and the times when they occur.

(*Answer.* (a) 5.76 km (b) 8.0 m/s (c) 3056 (d) 48 rad/s
(e) +0.08 m/s^2 at 2 min, −0.08 m/s^2 at 10 min.)

9. A cam is designed to raise a valve with a uniform acceleration of 100 m/s^2 lasting for 5 ms, followed immediately by a deceleration of 100 m/s^2 of similar duration. Draw the velocity–time graph. Hence find the maximum velocity of the valve and its total lift.

(*Answer.* 0.5 m/s, 2.5 mm.)

10. The armature of an electric motor requires 20 s to accelerate from rest to a speed of 1050 rev/min. After doing so, the motor is allowed to run at this speed for 2 min. The power is then switched off, and the armature turns through a further 700 rev before coming to rest.
Determine: (a) the initial acceleration of the armature; (b) the time taken for the armature to come to rest after the power is disconnected; (c) the final deceleration of the armature; (d) the total number of revolutions over the whole period.

(*Answer.* (a) 5.5 rad/s^2 (b) 80 s (c) 1.375 rad/s^2 (d) 2975.)

11. A rocket rises vertically with constant acceleration. After reaching a height of 1 km, the rocket is observed to rise from 1 km to 2 km in 1.3 s, and from 2 km to 3 km in 1.0 s.
Determine the acceleration of the rocket, and its velocity at the height of 3 km.

(*Answer.* 201 m/s^2, 1100 m/s.)

1. DYNAMICS

12. A car travelling at 25 km/h along a straight level road accelerates uniformly at 0.6 m/s^2 until its speed is 100 km/h. It maintains this speed for a period of time, and then decelerates uniformly at 2 m/s^2 until its velocity is zero. If the distance travelled by the car from the beginning of the acceleration period to finally coming to rest is 3 km, find the time of the constant velocity period.

(*Answer.* 79.4 s.)

13. A stone is projected vertically upwards with an initial velocity of 18 m/s. Assuming $g = 9.81 \text{ m/s}^2$, and neglecting air resistance, find; (a) the maximum height reached; (b) the time taken to reach maximum height; (c) the times at which the stone is at a height of 9 m.

(*Answer.* (a) 16.5 m (b) 1.835 s (c) 0.597 s and 3.072 s.)

14. A and B are two points rotating in circles, at constant speeds about the same axis O. The point A rotates at 15 rad/s in a circle of radius 20 mm, while B rotates in the same direction at 8 rad/s in a circle of 12 mm radius.
Find the velocity of A relative to B when the angle AOB is 60°.

(*Answer.* 0.265 m/s at 18° 16′ to the direction of motion of A.)

15. At noon, three ships, A, B, and C, lie on the same latitude. A is 100 km due west of B, and C is 200 km due east of B. The ship B is proceeding due north at 10 km/h, while A is sailing north-east at 20 km/h.
At what time will A and B lie on the same longitutude, and what then will be the distance between them?
What course and speed must the ship C maintain if it is to rendezvous with B at this time?

(*Answer.* 7.04 p.m., A is 29.43 km due north of B, 70° 32′ west of north at 30 km/h.)

16. A pit cage with a total mass of 1000 kg is at rest at the bottom of a mine shaft. The cage is raised with uniform acceleration, so that is rises 100 m in 20 s.
Calculate the tension in the cable.

(*Answer.* 10.3 kN.)

17. A body of mass 15 kg is at rest on a smooth plane inclined at 30° to the horizontal. When released, the body accelerates down the plane.
Calculate: (a) the normal reaction between the body and the

plane; (b) the acceleration of the body; (c) the distance travelled down the plane in 1 min.

(*Answer.* (*a*) 127.4 N (b) 4.905 m/s^2 (c) 8.829 km.)

18. A motor car, of total mass 1 tonne, is travelling at constant speed of 60 km/h up an incline of 1 in 30 against frictional resistances of 0.1 N/kg.
Calculate the tractive effort required to maintain this constant speed.
If the engine is suddenly switched off, what will be the time taken for the car to come at rest?

(*Answer.* 427 N, 39 s.)

19. The table of a planing machine has a mass of 600 kg. The power is shut off during operation and as a result the table comes to rest in 0.5 s after travelling a distance of 150 mm.
Estimate the force on the cutting tool, assuming this to be independent of speed. The coefficient of sliding friction between the table and the machine bed may be taken to be 0.1.

(*Answer.* 131.4 N.)

20. Masses of 12 kg and 18 kg are connected by a light inextensible string. The string is passed over a smooth peg, so that the masses hang down vertically on either side. If the system is then released, calculate its acceleration, and the tension in the string.

(*Answer.* 1.98 m/s^2, 141.3 N.)

21. A light inextensible string carrying masses of 5 kg and 4 kg, respectively, at each end is passed over a fixed steel pin of mass 1 kg. The axis of the pin is horizontal and the masses hang down vertically on either side. When the system is released, the larger mass is observed to fall from rest through a vertical height of 900 mm in 2 seconds. Calculate: (a) the total circumferential force of friction between pin and string; (b) the total vertical force required to support the pin during the motion.

(*Answer.* (a) 5.76 N (b) 97.65 N.)

22. A motor car has a mass of 1200 kg and is uniformly accelerated from rest to a speed of 72 km/h in a distance of 50 m on a level road. Assuming that the total resistances to motion amount to a force of 0.2 N/kg, determine: (a) the propulsive force of the vehicle; (b) the change in momentum.

(*Answer.* (a) 5.04 kN (b) 24 000 kg m/s.)

1. DYNAMICS

23. A locomotive of mass 100 tonne is used to draw a train of mass 400 tonne. Resistances to motion are equivalent to 0.1 N/kg for both locomotive and train. If the draw-bar pull between locomotive and train does not exceed 200 kN, determine: (a) the maximum acceleration which can be achieved on a level track; (b) the maximum gradient which can be ascended at constant speed; (c) the tractive effort exerted by the locomotive in each of these cases.

(*Answer.* (a) 0.4 m/s^2 (b) 1/24.5 (c) 250 kN in both cases.)

2. Forces and moments

2.1 Representation of forces by vectors

A force is a vector quantity, and as such possesses magnitude, direction, and sense. In specifying a force, therefore, all three must be given. The most convenient method is to represent the force by means of a vector, as in Fig. 2.1(b). If the point of application of a force is important, it may be shown on a space diagram, as in Fig. 2.1(a).

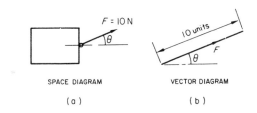

SPACE DIAGRAM   VECTOR DIAGRAM

(a)   (b)

Figure 2.1

The total effect, or *resultant*, of a number of forces acting on a body may be determined by vector addition, as explained in Chapter 1. Conversely, a single force may be resolved into components (Section 1.3), such that these components have the same total effect as the original force. It is often convenient to replace a force by its two components at right angles, and, in this respect, note should be taken of Eqs 1.6 and 1.7.

2.2 Coplanar forces

Forces whose lines of action all lie in the same plane are called 'coplanar forces'. The following laws relating to coplanar forces are of importance and should be noted carefully. However, it must also be remembered that these laws are applicable only to two–dimensional problems.

1. *The line of action of the resultant of any two coplanar forces must*

41

pass through the point of intersection of the lines of action of the two forces.

2. If any number of coplanar forces act on a body and are not in equilibrium, then they can always be reduced to a single resultant force and a couple (see Section 2.4).

3. If three forces acting on a body are in equilibrium, then their lines of action must be concurrent, that is, they must all pass through the same point.

2.3 The moment of a force

When a force is applied to a body, the effect may be either to cause the body to move in a straight line, or to cause it to rotate, or both. The turning effect of a force is called the *moment* of the force about the axis of rotation. The turning effect or moment of a force about a point is dependent on two quantities: the magnitude of the force, and the perpendicular distance of the point from the line of action of the force.

Figure 2.2

If either of these quantities is increased, the moment is increased. Therefore, with reference to Fig. 2.2,

$$\text{moment of a force, } F, \text{ about a point } O = F \times x$$

The distance x is often referred to as the 'moment arm'.

A common example of the turning effect of a force is when a door is rotated about its hinge. The door handle is always placed as far from the hinge as possible in order to reduce the force required for a given turning effect.

Where more than one force acts on a body, the total turning effect is the algebraic sum of the moments of the forces. For example, suppose it is required to calculate the resultant moment about the pivot O of the forces shown acting on the bell-crank lever in Fig. 2.3, where $AO = 100$ mm and $OC = BC = 20$ mm. The force of 10 N tends to rotate the lever clockwise, whereas the other tend to rotate the lever anticlockwise. Clearly, the 10 N force is in opposition to the other two and must therefore be regarded as negative.

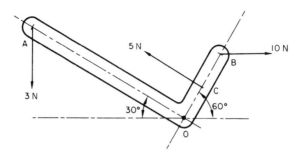

Figure 2.3

Total moment about O

$$= 3(\text{AO} \cos 30°) + 5(\text{OC}) - 10(\text{OB} \sin 60°)$$

$$= 3(0.100 \cos 30°) + 5(0.020) - 10(0.040 \sin 60°) \text{ Nm}$$

$$= 0.2598 + 0.100 - 0.3464 \text{ N m}$$

$$= 0.0134 \text{ N m, in an anticlockwise sense.}$$

Note that the sense as well as the magnitude of the total moment is given, and that the unit of a moment is the product of the force unit, the newton (N), and the unit of length, the metre (m).

2.4 The couple

When two equal and opposite forces, not in the same straight line, act on a body, their moment about *any* point in the plane is always the same. Two such forces, as in Fig. 2.4, are said to form a *couple*. The moment of a couple is frequently referred to as a 'torque'.

With reference to Fig. 2.4,

total moment of the forces about $O = F(d + x) - Fx$

$$= Fd(\text{clockwise}) \quad (2.1)$$

The total moment of the couple about O is thus independent of the distance x, and it follows that O may be anywhere in the plane without affecting the magnitude of the couple.

Figure 2.4

2.5 Conditions of equilibrium for coplanar forces

A body is said to be in equilibrium when the total effect of all the forces acting on the body is zero. A body which is in the state of equilibrium will therefore have no tendency either to move in a straight line or to rotate.

Two conditions are therefore essential for equilibrium:

1. *The vector sum of all the forces acting on the body must be zero;*
2. *The algebraic sum of the moments about any point of all the forces acting on the body must be zero.*

If it is required to establish the equilibrium of a body, *both* conditions must be satisfied.

Conversely, if a body is known to be in equilibrium, then these conditions must apply, and their application is useful in the determination of unknown forces.

Following directly from these conditions of equilibrium are two principles widely used in problems involving static equilibrium. These are the principle of the polygon of forces, and the principle of moments.

2.6 The polygon of forces

If any number of coplanar forces acting on a body are in equilibrium, they may be represented in magnitude and direction by the sides of a closed polygon, taken in order.

This, of course, is merely a restatement of the first condition of equilibrium, since if the vector sum is zero, the force vector diagram must indeed form a closed polygon.

The principle is demonstrated in Fig. 2.5 which shows a space

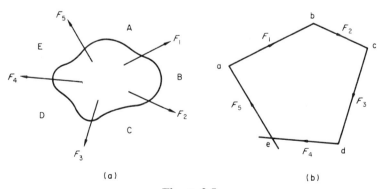

(a)   (b)

Figure 2.5

diagram depicting five forces acting on a body (Fig. 2.5(a)), and the corresponding force vector diagram (Fig. 2.5(b)). Note that, to draw the vector diagram, only three of the forces need to be known in magnitude, for when vectors **ab**, **bc**, and **cd**, have been drawn to represent F_1, F_2, and F_3, respectively, the directions alone of F_4 and F_5 are sufficient to locate the point e. Hence, if F_4 and F_5 are unknown in magnitude, they can be determined from the force polygon. In general, the force polygon may be drawn provided there are no more than two forces unknown in magnitude.

Bow's notation

Figure 2.5 also demonstrates the application of Bow's notation. On the space diagram, the spaces between the forces are lettered using *capital* letters. The force F_1 may then be referred to as the force AB, F_2 as the force BC, etc. Corresponding *small* letters are then used to designate the vectors in the force polygon; the force AB is therefore represented by the vector **ab**. The use of this notation will be found to be most effective in the construction and interpretation of force polygons.

2.7 The principle of moments

If any number of coplanar forces acting on a body are in equilibrium, the algebraic sum of the moments of these forces about any point in the plane must be zero.

This is, of course, the second condition of equilibrium and may also be stated in the form:

$$\begin{matrix} \text{total clockwise moment} \\ \text{about some point} \end{matrix} = \begin{matrix} \text{total anticlockwise moment} \\ \text{about the same point} \end{matrix}$$

(2.2)

2.8 Simply supported beams

A beam is a member designed to carry transverse loads, that is, loads perpendicular to the axis of the member. Usually, the beam is mounted horizontally and carries vertically applied loads. Its purpose is to allow these loads to be supported by means of reaction forces remote from the load positions. Very often, the loads are gravitational forces due to the weight of some body which is being maintained in position by the beam.

If the applied loads are vertical, the reaction forces must also be vertical, and the first condition of equilibrium reduces to the simple statement that

| the sum of the upward forces | the sum of the downward forces |
| acting on the beam | acting on the beam |

(2.3)

A simply supported beam is one which is considered to rest on knife-edge supports. A minimum of two such supports is required to maintain the beam in equilibrium. Because there are two unknown support reactions, Eq. 2.3 will not, by itself, yield their magnitudes, but application of the principle of moments provides a further equation enabling them to be determined. Thus, the conditions of equilibrium provide *two* equations from which *two* unknown support reactions may be found. For this reason, a beam having only two simple supports is said to be 'statically determinate'.

In fact, by selecting one of the supports as the point about which moments are taken, the principle of moments gives the reaction at the other support directly. A second application of the moments equation, using the other support as the pivot, will complete the investigation. This leaves Eq. 2.3 as a useful check on the calculation.

Consider, for example, the simply supported beam in Fig. 2.6. The unknown support reaction, R_E, has zero moment about the point E so that, taking E as the pivot, the principle of moments will provide an equation containing only one unknown, the reaction R_A. Thus, taking moments about E,

$$R_A \times 8 = (3 \times 6) + (9 \times 3) + (5 \times 1) \text{ kN m}$$
$$= \quad 18 \quad + \quad 27 \quad + \quad 5 \text{ kN m}$$
$$R_A = \frac{50}{8} = 6.25 \text{ kN}$$

In a similar manner, the reaction R_E may be determined, independently, by taking moments about point A.

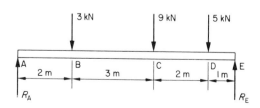

Figure 2.6

Taking moments about A,

$$R_E \times 8 = (3 \times 2) + (9 \times 5) + (5 \times 7) \text{ kN m}$$
$$= \quad 6 \quad + \quad 45 \quad + \quad 35 \quad \text{ kN m}$$
$$R_E = \frac{86}{8} = 10.75 \text{ kN}$$

The two reactions, R_A and R_E, have each been found by independent calculations. To verify the results, the following check can be carried out:

total upward force $= R_A + R_E = 6.25 + 10.75 = 17 \text{ kN}$

total downward force $= 3 + 9 + 5 = 17 \text{ kN}$

which conforms with the requirements of Eq. 2.3.

Another example is shown in Fig. 2.7, which depicts a simply supported beam with overhanging ends. Again, the support points are used as the pivots in the respective moments equations.

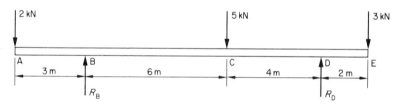

Figure 2.7

Referring to Fig. 2.7, take moments about D.

Clockwise moments about D = anticlockwise moments about D

$$(R_B \times 10) + (3 \times 2) = (2 \times 13) + (5 \times 4) \text{ kN m}$$
$$10R_B + 6 = 26 + 20 \text{ kN m}$$
$$10R_B = 26 + 20 - 6 \text{ kN m}$$
$$R_B = \frac{40}{10} = 4 \text{ kN}$$

Taking moments about B,

clockwise moments about B = anticlockwise moments about B

$$(5 \times 6) + (3 \times 12) = (R_D \times 10) + (2 \times 3) \text{ kNm}$$
$$30 + 36 \quad = 10R_D + 6 \text{ kN m}$$

47

Rearranging, $\qquad 10R_D = 30 + 36 - 6 \text{ kN m}$

$$R_D = \frac{60}{10} = 6 \text{ kN}$$

To verify these calculations,

total upward force $= R_B + R_D = 4 + 6 = 10 \text{ kN}$

total downward force $= 2 + 5 + 3 = 10 \text{ kN}$

which confirms that no mistake has been made in the moments calculations.

2.9 The simple or articulated framework

If two rigid members are connected by means of a frictionless pin-joint, then, although inseparable, each member is free to rotate relative to the other. Such joints are described as articulated joints and are incapable of resisting a torque or moment. Because of this, the only way in which force may be transmitted from one member to the other, while the members are in static equilibrium, is by means of a force whose line of action passes through the pin. Any other line of action would produce a turning moment about the pin, which the joint would be unable to resist, and rotation would occur. Thus, forces of interaction between members connected by pin-joints must pass through the pin.

By using only pin-joints, it is possible to build up a framework whose geometry will remain appreciably unchanged when subjected to loads. The basic example of this is shown in Fig. 2.8, in which three members are connected by pin-joints to form a triangular frame. If the members are rigid, the sides of the triangle are fixed in length and the frame cannot distort. Nevertheless, it still remains true that the pin-joints at A, B, and C cannot resist any moment.

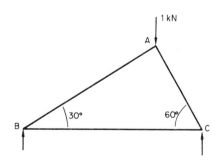

Figure 2.8

Frames of this type, employing only pin-joints, are referred to as 'simple frameworks'.

2.10 Forces acting on a member

Consider the equilibrium of a single member of a simple framework. If the force due to gravity is neglected, only two forces will act on the member: these are the forces which act at the pin-joints at each end of the member. If two forces maintain a body in static equilibrium, they must be equal and opposite and must lie in the same straight line. Since these forces must also pass through the pin at each end, it follows that the common line of action of the forces is the straight line connecting these pins. Figure 2.9 illustrates this principle for a curved member as well as for a straight member.

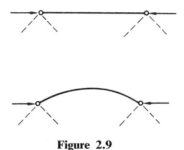

Figure 2.9

For straight members, the common line of action coincides with the axis of the member. Such members, therefore, are subjected only to forces which tend to stretch or to compress the member and which have no traverse components (i.e., components perpendicular to the axis). Forces of this type are called *direct* loads. Those tending to stretch the member are described as *tensile* while those tending to compress are called *compressive*. The normal convention is to regard tensile loads as positive and compressive loads as negative. A member which is subjected to a direct tensile load is called a *tie*, since its function is to hold together two points in a structure. A member subjected to a direct compressive load is called a *strut*, its function being to keep two points apart.

2.11 Forces acting on a pin-joint

Figure 2.10 shows four members of a simple frame meeting at a pin-joint. Each member will exert a force on the pin and these forces will be equal and opposite to the forces applied to the

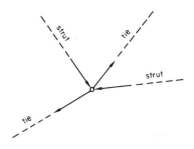

Figure 2.10

respective members. Thus, those members which are ties will exert forces on the pin radiating outwards from the pin, while those members which are struts will exert forces converging inwards on the pin.

Since the members of a simple framework carry only direct loads, i.e., acting along the axis of the member, the forces acting on the pin, which are equal and opposite, are known in direction. Provided no more than two are unknown in magnitude, the polygon of forces may be drawn to represent the equilibrium of these forces (see Section 2.6). From this diagram, the two unknown forces may be determined. By considering, in this way, the equilibrium of the forces acting *on the pin*, the magnitudes and senses of the forces in the members may be found.

2.12 The reciprocal diagram for a simple framework

As a simple example, consider the triangluar framework of Fig. 2.11. There are three pin-joints, and at one of them, joint A, three forces act on the pin, only two of which are unknown in magnitude. All three forces are known in direction, the applied load of 1 kN being vertical and the forces applied to the pin by the members AB and AC being directed along the axes of these members. The force polygon representing their equilibrium is shown in Fig. 2.11(a), Bow's notation having been used (see Section 2.6).

It is apparent from Fig. 2.11(a) that the force exerted on the pin at A by member AC has the magnitude, direction, and sense of vector **yz**; while the force exerted on the pin at A by member AB has the magnitude, direction, and sense of vector **zx**. Both AB and AC are pushing upwards on the pin and are therefore struts.

If the member AB is pushing upwards on A with the force **zx**, it must be pushing downwards on B with the equal and opposite force **xz**. Thus, at B, there now exists a system of three forces, only two of

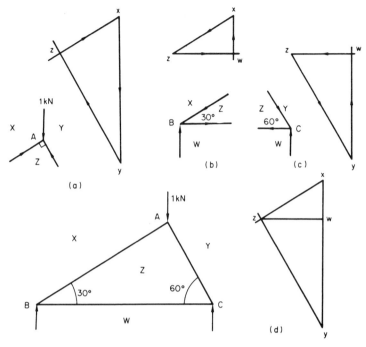

Figure 2.11

which are unknown in magnitude, and the force polygon representing the equilibrium of the forces acting on B may be drawn. This is
shown in Fig. 2.11(b). Bow's notation has again been used, and it
should be noticed that, since the force exerted on B by the member
AB is **xz**, the appropriate letters have been used in the space
diagram of Fig. 2.11(b). These letters appear in the same relative
positions as they did in Fig. 2.11(a), provided they are read with the
same sense of rotation (in this case clockwise) about the pin; i.e., X–
Z–W in Fig. 2.11(b) and X–Y–Z in Fig. 2.11(a). From the force
diagram of Fig. 2.11(b), the vertical support reaction at B is given by
vector **wx**, while vector **zw** reveals the magnitude and sense of the
force in member BC. BC is seen to be a tie.

Figure 2.11(c) shows the space and force diagrams for the forces
acting on the pin at C. This force polygon is not essential because
the forces in members AB and AC are obtainable from Fig. 2.11(a),
and the force in member BC from Fig, 2.11(b), but it is given in
order to complete the picture.

Careful examination of the force vector diagrams of Fig. 2.11(a),
(b), and (c) reveals that the vectors representing the forces in the

members have each been drawn twice. This duplication of effort can be avoided by combining all three force polygons into a single force diagram, as shown in Fig. 2.11(d). This combined diagram is called the *reciprocal* diagram for the frame.

In combining the force diagrams in this way, it becomes necessary to omit the arrows indicating the sense of the vectors, since the sense of each vector may be taken either way, depending on which joint is being considered. It is therefore imperative to adopt a *consistent* method for 'reading' the forces in the space diagram. At each pin-joint, the letters allocated to spaces in accordance with Bow's notation should be read with the same sense of rotation. For convenience a clockwise sense has been adhered to in this book so that, in Fig. 2.11(d) for example, the forces at A are: the load XY (vector **xy**); YZ (vector **yz**); and ZX (vector **zx**). Similarly, at joint B the forces are XZ (vector **xz**), ZW (vector **zw**), and WX (vector **wx**); and at joint C, the forces are ZY (vector **zy**), YW (vector **yw**), and WZ (vector **wz**).

The reciprocal diagram of Fig. 2.11(d) is the result of combining three polygons of forces. It should be noticed that a fourth closed polygon is present in the diagram. This is the polygon representing the equilibrium of the external forces applied to the frame. In this case, the applied load, as represented by vector **xy**, is balanced by the two support reactions, as represented by **yw** and **wx**. From the diagram,

$$\mathbf{xy} + \mathbf{yw} + \mathbf{wx} = 0$$

When the construction of a reciprocal diagram is completed, the external force polygon should always be checked for correct closure. This takes very little time, and will usually reveal the existence of any error in the diagram.

The following general rules should be followed when drawing the reciprocal diagram for a simple framework.

(a) Draw the space diagram for the frame, ensuring that all external forces, including reactions at supports, have been shown.

(b) Allocate a *capital* letter to each space separating the adjacent forces. Perhaps the best method is first to letter the spaces between external loads around the periphery of the frame, and then to letter the spaces between the various members. Letters should be chosen which do not conflict with those already used to designate pin-joints.

(c) Look for a pin-joint at which there are no more than two forces unknown in magnitude. If no such joint exists, it may be necessary to calculate an unknown support reaction by considering the equilibrium of the frame as a whole and using the principle of moments.

(d) Draw the force polygon for this joint, using Bow's notation and reading the lettered spaces in a clockwise manner around the joint. Arrows should be omitted from the force vectors, and corresponding *small* letters should be used to designate them. This determines the magnitude and sense of the two unknown forces.

(e) Indicate on the space diagram, by means of appropriate arrows, the forces exerted by the members on the pin-joint, and indicate similarly the presence of an equal and opposite force at the other end of each member.

(f) Repeat (c), (d), and (e) until the reciprocal diagram is complete.

If the forces in all the members are required, then these are best presented in a tabulated form. The table should classify each member as a 'tie' or a 'strut', as well as giving the magnitude of the force it carries.

Worked examples

1. Figure 2.12(a) shows a link AB which is acted upon by a horizontal and a vertical force at A, and a single force at B acting in the direction shown.

Determine the line of action, the magnitude, the direction, and the sense of the resultant of these forces.

The forces applied at A are first combined into a single resultant, as shown in Fig. 2.12(b). This resultant and the force at B intersect at the point O. Since there are now only two forces acting, their resultant must pass through O, and combining these into a single, final resultant gives:

magnitude of the resultant = 1480 N = 1.48 kN

direction and sense = 39° to AB, upwards

the line of action passes through C, where AC = 0.135 m

2. Find the magnitude and direction of the force at B necessary to maintain the equilibrium of the link AGB (Fig. 2.13). Find also the force due to gravity acting on the link.

Since the link is in equilibrium under the action of three forces, the force at B must be concurrent with the forces at A and G; that is, the force at B must pass through O (Fig. 2.14).

2. FORCES AND MOMENTS

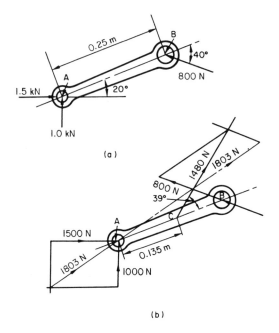

(a)

(b)

Figure 2.12

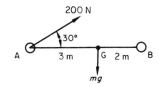

Figure 2.13

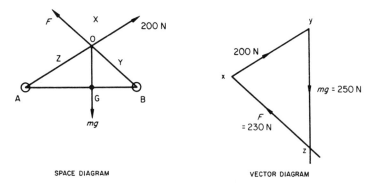

SPACE DIAGRAM   VECTOR DIAGRAM

Figure 2.14

As the directions of all three forces are known, Bow's notation may be applied and the polygon of forces drawn.

From the vector diagram of Fig. 2.14,

force at $B = \mathbf{zx} = 230$ N at $41.5°$ to the horizontal,

force of gravity on the link $= \mathbf{yz} = 250$ N

3. A mass of 100 kg is supported by means of a bell-crank lever, as shown in Fig. 2.15. Determine the magnitude of the force F

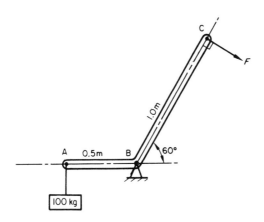

Figure 2.15

required to maintain equilibrium. Find also the magnitude and direction of the reaction at the pivot B.

Assuming $g = 10$ m/s², gravitational force on load $= mg = 1000$ N. Taking moments about B,

clockwise moment = anticlockwise moment

$$F(1.0) = 1000(0.5) \text{ N m}$$

$$= 500 \text{ N}$$

Since there are only three forces acting on the lever, the reaction R must pass through the intersection of the forces at A and C, as shown in Fig. 2.16.

From the vector diagram, $R = 1323$ N at $19° 6'$ to the vertical.

4. Determine the magnitudes of the reactions at the supports for the loaded beam shown in Fig. 2.17.

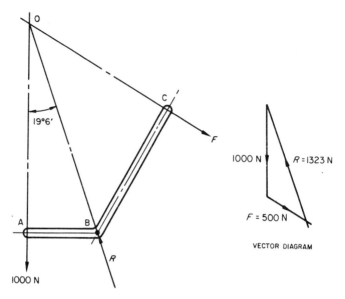

Figure 2.16

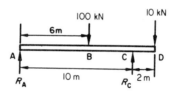

Figure 2.17

Take moments about A, so that the moment of the force R_A is zero.

total clockwise moment = total anticlockwise moment

$$100(6) + 10(12) = R_C(10) \text{ kN m}$$
$$600 + 120 = 10 \, R_C \text{ kN m}$$
$$R_C = 72 \text{ kN}$$

Take moments about C, so that the moment of the force R_C is zero.

total clockwise moment = total anticlockwise moment

$$R_A(10) + 10(2) = 100(4) \text{ kN m}$$
$$10 \, R_A = 400 - 20 \text{ kN m}$$
$$R_A = 38 \text{ kN}$$

WORKED EXAMPLES

Check: total upward force $= R_A + R_C = 72 + 38 = 110$ kN

total downward force $= 100 + 10 = 110$ kN.

5. A simple framework ABCD, consisting of five members, is shown in Fig. 2.18(a). The frame is hinged at A, and supported on rollers at D, thereby ensuring a vertical reaction there. Vertical loads of 3 kN and 2 kN are supported at B and C, respectively.

Draw the reciprocal diagram for the framework, and hence determine the load carried by each member. Complete a table showing the magnitudes of the loads, and the function of each member.

The space diagram of Fig. 2.18(a) is lettered in accordance with Bow's notation.

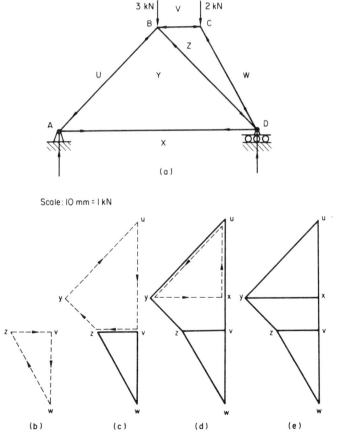

Figure 2.18

57

Consider first the equilibrium of the framework under the action of the four external forces. Because the point is supported on rollers, no horizontal component of force can be reacted at D, so that the reaction at D must be vertical. Furthermore, since the loads at B and C are also vertical, the reaction at A will be vertical, there being no horizontal component of any external force for this hinge to react.

The joint C is the only one at which there are no more than two forces unknown in magnitude. The force polygon demonstrating the equilibrium of the forces acting on the pin at C is therefore drawn, and this is shown dotted in Fig. 2.18(b). The sense of these forces is immediately transferred to the members in the space diagram at C. Equal and opposite forces may then be indicated at the other ends of members CB and CD.

The force polygon for joint B may then be added, and this is shown dotted in Fig. 2.18(c). Again, the sense of each force is transferred to the space diagram at B, and forces of opposite sense indicated at the other ends of members BA and BD.

The force polygon for joint A may then be added, as indicated by the dotted lines in Fig. 2.18(d), and again the appropriate sense of the forces indicated in the space diagram.

Figures 2.18(b), (c), and (d) are, of course, only given for explanatory purposes. In practice, only the complete reciprocal diagram (Fig. 2.18(e)) need be drawn. From the reciprocal diagram, and the arrows on the space diagram, the following table may be drawn up:

Member	Type	Force (kN)
AB	strut	3.0
BC	strut	1.2
CD	strut	2.3
DA	tie	2.1
BD	strut	1.3

6. Figure 2.19 shows the space and reciprocal diagrams for a simple framework. From the reciprocal diagram, deduce the magnitude of the forces in members EF, FG, and GH, and whether they are ties or struts.

Since Bow's notation has been used, it is clear that the vertical *downward* load of 2 kN is represented by vector **ab**. This establishes the scale of the diagram and also the fact that the letters in the space diagram have been read in a *clockwise* sense.

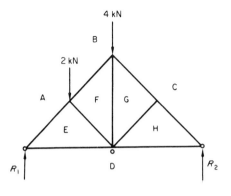

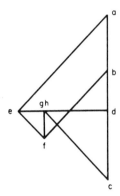

Figure 2.19

Consider the forces acting on the pin at the junction marked O. Reading the letters clockwise around this joint,

force exerted on O by the member EF = **ef** = 1.414 kN

The sense of this force shows the member to be pushing down on O, so that EF is a strut.

Force exerted on O by the member FG = **fg** = 1.0 kN

The sense of this force shows the member to be pulling upwards on O, so that FG is a tie.

Force exerted on O by member GH = **gh** = 0 (since g and h coincide)

7. Draw the force diagram for the cantilever frame shown in Fig. 2.20(a). Tabulate the magnitudes of the forces in each member, at

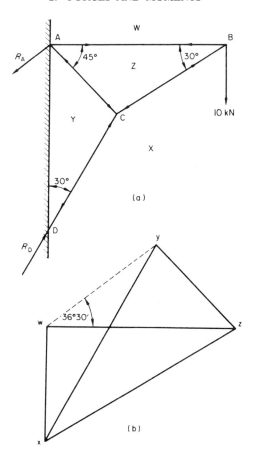

Figure 2.20

the same time stating whether they are ties or struts. Find also the magnitude and direction of the reactions at the wall.

Bow's notation is first applied, in the usual way. The joint B must be considered first, since this is the only one at which there are no more than two unknown forces.

By considering the equilibrium of the forces at B, the force polygon **wx, xz, zw** may be drawn. This may be followed by the force polygon for joint C (**zx, xy, yz**). Note that, until the force polygon for joint C has been drawn, there are *three* unknowns at A: the magnitude of the force in AC; the magnitude of the reaction R_A; and the *direction* of the reaction R_A. The completed reciprocal diagram is shown in Fig. 2.20(b).

The required information may be obtained from this diagram, and is tabulated below.

Member	Type	Force (kN)
AB	tie	17.3
BC	strut	20.0
CD	strut	20.0
AC	strut	10.4

The reaction at $A = R_A = \mathbf{yw} = 12.2$ kN at $36°\ 30'$ to the horizontal.
The reaction at $D = R_D = \mathbf{xy} = 20.0$ kN at $30°$ to the vertical.

8. A pin-jointed structure is loaded and supported as shown in Fig. 2.21(a). Draw the reciprocal diagram, and hence find the nature and magnitude of the forces in members AB, BC, and CD.

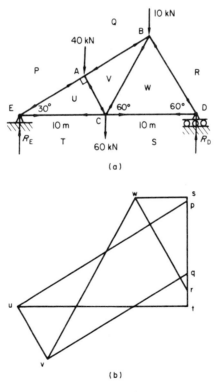

(a)

(b)

Figure 2.21

In this case, there are more than two unknown forces at every joint. It is necessary, therefore, to determine one of the reactions by considering, first, the equilibrium of the frame as a whole.

Taking moments about E,

$$R_D \times 20 = (60 \times 10) + (10 \times 15) + (40 \times 7.5)$$
$$R_D = (600 + 150 + 300)/20 = 52.5 \text{ kN}$$

The force polygon for joint D may now be drawn (**rs, sw, wr**). This is followed by the force polygon for joint B (**qr, rw, wv, vq**), the force polygons for joint A and joint C, and, finally, the force polygon for joint E. The completed reciprocal diagram is shown in Fig. 2.21(b). From the reciprocal diagram:

$$\text{compressive force in AB} = \mathbf{qv} = 94 \text{ kN}$$
$$\text{tensile force in BC} = \mathbf{vw} = 103 \text{ kN}$$
$$\text{tensile force in CD} = \mathbf{ws} = 30.3 \text{ kN}$$

Problems

1. A uniform rod is 2 m long and the force due to gravity acting on it is 300 N. One end of the rod is hinged to the floor so that it may rotate in a vertical plane. The other end of the rod is tied to a point on the ceiling vertically above the hinge by means of a rope 2.5 m long. The vertical height of the ceiling above the floor is 3 m.

Determine the magnitude and direction of the reaction at the hinge and the magnitude of the tension in the rope. Neglect the gravitational force on the rope.

(*Answer.* 222 N at 21° 50′ to the vertical, 125 N.)

2. A garden roller has a diameter of 0.60 m, and the force due to gravity acting upon it is 750 N. The roller is drawn along a level path until it meets a step 100 mm high. Assuming the handle of the roller to be inclined at 30° to the horizontal, what is the least force which must be applied directly to the handle to cause the roller to mount the step?

(*Answer.* 588.6 N.)

3. A mass of 50 kg lies on a smooth plane inclined at 25° to the horizontal, and is maintained in a state of equilibrium by a force *F*. Determine the magnitude of *F* and the normal reaction between the plane and the mass (a) if *F* is horizontal (b) if *F* is parallel to the plane.
Assume $g = 10 \text{ m/s}^2$.

(*Answer.* (a) $F = 233$ N, $R_N = 552$ N (b) $F = 211$ N, $R_N = 452$ N.)

PROBLEMS

4. ABCD is a rectangle in which AB = 1 m and BC = 2 m. A force of 20 N acts along the side AB, in the sense from A to B; a force of 30 N acts along the diagonal AC, in the sense from A to C; a force of 10 N acts along the side AD, in the sense from A to D; and a force of 20 N acts along the side DC, in the sense from D to C.

Determine the magnitude and direction of the resultant of these forces, and the distance from A that its line of action cuts the side AD.

(*Answer.* 65 N at $55\frac{1}{2}°$ to AD, 0.75 m.)

5. A beam ABCDEF is simply supported at B and E. AB = 2 m; BC = 5 m; CD = 3 m; DE = EF = 2 m. Transverse loads of 5 kN, 10 kN, 8 kN, and 3 kN, respectively, are applied at A, C, D, and F.

Calculate the reactions at the supports.

(*Answer.* R_B = 12 kN, R_E = 14 kN.)

6. Draw the reciprocal diagram for the simple framework of Fig. 2.22 and hence determine the magnitudes of the forces in all the members, and the function fulfilled by each member. Tabulate your results. What are the magnitudes and directions of the support reactions?

(*Answer.* F_{AB} = 8.66 kN, F_{BC} = F_{CD} = 10 kN, all ties;

F_{AE} = 4.33 kN, F_{BE} = 5 kN, F_{CE} = F_{DE} = 10 kN, all struts;

R_A = 7.5 kN, vertically downwards;

R_E = 17.5 kN, vertically upwards.)

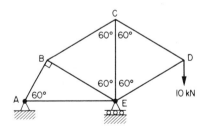

Figure 2.22

7. Figure 2.23 shows a pin-jointed structure carrying vertical loads of 2 kN and 4 kN, respectively, at B and C. Assuming the

63

2. FORCES AND MOMENTS

reactions at A and E to be vertical, determine the nature and magnitude of the forces in FC, CG, and GD.

(*Answer.* $F_{FC} = 2.12$ kN, compression; $F_{CG} = 2.5$ kN, compression; $F_{GD} = 3.535$ kN, tension.)

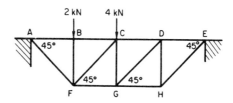

Figure 2.23

8. The cantilever framework of Fig. 2.24 carries equal loads of 10 kN at B and C. Assuming pin-joints throughout, find the nature and magnitude of the forces in members AB, BE, and ED. Find, also, the magnitude and direction of the reactions at A and F.

(*Answer.* $F_{AB} = 17.32$ kN, tension;

$\quad$ $F_{BE} = 17.32$ kN, compression;

$\quad$ $F_{ED} = 10$ kN, compression;

$\quad$ $R_A = 22.91$ kN, upwards and to the left, at 19° 6' to the horizontal;

$\quad$ $R_F = 25$ kN, upwards and to the right, at 30° to the horizontal.)

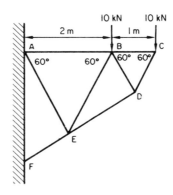

Figure 2.24

9. Determine the nature and magnitude of the forces in the members AB, BF, and FE, of the simple framework shown in Fig. 2.25. Find also the magnitude and direction of the support reactions.

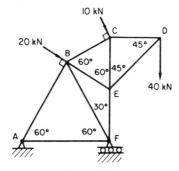

Figure 2.25

(*Answer.* $F_{AB} = 45$ kN, tension; $F_{BF} = 0$, $F_{FE} = 98$ kN, compression;
$R_A = 45$ kN, downwards and in the direction of BA;
$R_F = 98$ kN, vertically upwards.)

3. Stress and strain

3.1 Direct stress

In Section 2.10, a direct load was defined as a force which tends to stretch or compress a member, and which has no transverse component. In the context of Section 2.10, this definition refers to a straight member such as those of Fig. 3.1. A more general definition, referring to a body of any shape, would describe a direct load as one whose direction was perpendicular to the cross-sectional area (c.s.a.) resisting fracture.

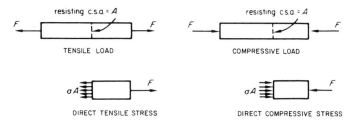

Figure 3.1

For example, the tensile load of Fig. 3.1 is tending to pull apart the two ends of the member. This is prevented by the molecular bond along all planes at right angles to the applied load. A typical plane resisting fracture is indicated by the dotted line. Such a plane divides the body into two parts, which are evidently held together by forces of attachment distributed in some way across the section. These internal forces constitute a state of *stress*, which, in this case, is a direct stress since their direction is perpendicular to the section.

The way in which the forces of attachment are distributed across a transverse plane may, in general, vary depending on how the load is applied. However, for the cases of simple tension and compression, shown in Fig. 3.1, it is reasonable to assume a uniform distribution of these forces, provided the line of action of the applied load coincides with the centre of area of the cross-section. This assumption is borne out in practice, except perhaps at sections near the ends of the member. Thus, each unit of area of the section carries an equal share of the load, and it is useful to define this as the *intensity of stress:*

intensity of stress σ = force per unit area of section = F/A

(3.1)

which therefore has the units N/m^2.

The intensity of stress, more often referred to as simply 'the stress', does not necessarily mean 'total load/total area' (which would be described as average stress) but can refer to a very small area of the section. Thus, even in cases where the stress varies in intensity across the section, a value for the 'force/unit area' may be quoted for any given point.

A direct stress may be either tensile or compressive depending on the sense of the applied load. The usual convention is to regard a tensile stress as positive and a compressive stress as negative. The magnitude and sense of a direct stress may normally be found by imagining the body to be 'cut' by a transverse plane, as in Fig. 3.1, and considering the equilibrium of one part of the body. With reference to Fig. 3.1,

total force on cut face due to stress = the applied load

$$\sigma A = F$$

which is only another form of Eq. 3.1.

3.2 Direct strain

When the material of a body is in a state of stress, deformation takes place and the size and shape of the body are changed. The manner of deformation will depend on how the body is loaded, but a simple tension member tends to stretch and a simple compression member tends to contract. If the member has a uniform cross-sectional area, the intensity of stress will be the same throughout its length, so that each unit of length will extend or contract by the same amount. The total change in length, corresponding to a given stress, will thus depend on the original length of the member.

Deformation due to an internal state of stress is called *strain.* Any measurement of strain must be related to the original dimension involved, e.g., length. In general,

intensity of strain, ε = deformation/unit of original dimension

(3.2)

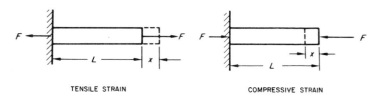

TENSILE STRAIN   COMPRESSIVE STRAIN

Figure 3.2

For simple tension or compression (Fig. 3.2), this becomes

intensity of strain, ε = change in length/original length = x/L

(3.3)

where x is the extension or compression of the member.

Again, this is usually referred to as simply 'the strain'. Since strain is the ratio between two lengths, it is dimensionless: it is, however, often expressed as a percentage.

3.3 Hooke's law

Engineering materials must, of necessity, possess the property of *elasticity*. This is the property which allows a piece of the material to regain its original size and shape when the forces producing a state of strain are removed. If a bar of elastic material, of uniform cross-section, is loaded progressively in tension, it will be found that, up to a point, the corresponding extensions will be proportional to the applied loads. This is Hooke's law. However, to be meaningful, loads and extensions must be related to a particular bar of known cross-sectional area and length. A more general statement of this law may be made in terms of the stress and strain in the material of the bar.

Within the limit of proportionality, the strain is directly proportional to the stress producing it.

The graph of stress against strain will thus be a straight line passing through the origin, as shown in Fig. 3.3.

The slope of this graph = stress/strain = a constant for a given material. This constant is known as *Young's modulus of elasticity* and is always denoted by E.

Young's modulus of elasticity,

$$E = \frac{\text{stress}}{\text{strain}} = \text{the slope of the stress–strain graph} \quad (3.4)$$

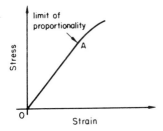

Figure 3.3

The value of E for any given material can only be obtained by carrying out tests on specimens of the material.

For mild steel, $E = 200 \times 10^9 \text{ N/m}^2 = 200 \text{ GN/m}^2$

For aluminium, $E = 70 \times 10^9 \text{ N/m}^2 = 70 \text{ GN/m}^2$

Notice that, since strain is a dimensionless quantity, E has the same units as stress. E could in fact be defined as the stress required to produce unit strain, but the concept is unreal, since such a stress would exceed both the limit of proportionality and the ultimate strength of the material by some considerable margin.

Hooke's law provides a means by which the extension, or compression, of a member may be calculated. From Eq. 3.4,

$$\text{strain} = \frac{\text{stress}}{E}$$

Substituting for stress and strain from Eqs 3.1 and 3.3, we get

$$\frac{x}{L} = \frac{F/A}{E}$$

$$x = \frac{FL}{EA} \tag{3.5}$$

3.4 Load–extension diagrams

It is obviously necessary, for design purposes, to know the value of Young's modulus for any material which is to be used for engineering purposes. Other properties of the material are also important; these include the greatest stress the material can withstand without fracturing, and the stress corresponding to the limit of proportionality.

To obtain this, and other information, a specimen of the material is produced in the form shown in Fig. 3.4. The working length of such a specimen is called 'the gauge length', and to this is attached an instrument capable of measuring small variations in this length.

3. STRESS AND STRAIN

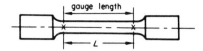

Figure 3.4

This instrument is called an extensometer. The enlarged ends of the specimen are clamped in the jaws of a testing machine, which stretches the specimen at a controlled rate. For progressively increasing amounts of extension, as indicated by the extensometer, the tensile load carried by the specimen is measured by means of a simple beam-balance technique, which is illustrated diagrammatically in Fig. 3.5. A tensile test of this nature may be continued until the specimen fractures, but it will be necessary to remove the extensometer (to avoid damaging it) soon after the limit of proportionality is reached, and thereafter to use a less sophisticated method of measuring the extension. The results obtained from such a test may then be used to plot a graph showing the variation of load with extension.

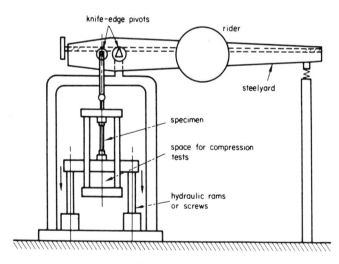

Figure 3.5

If a mild-steel specimen is tested in this way, the resulting graph will be similar to that of Fig. 3.6. From O to A the graph is linear, showing that Hooke's law applies, so that A is the *limit of proportionality*. Soon afterwards, a point B is reached, called the *elastic limit*, which represents the maximum elastic deformation of which

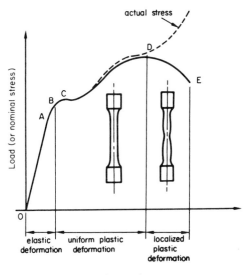

Figure 3.6

the material is capable. Up to this point, the extension will completely disappear when the load is removed. If, however, the elastic limit is exceeded, the material experiences *plastic** deformation, which means that when the load is removed the extension does not completely disappear and the specimen is left with a 'permament set'. At C, the specimen undergoes a sudden, and relatively appreciable, increase in length without any corresponding increase in load, and this is known as the *yield point.* This phenomenon of 'yielding' is peculiar to ferrous materials, particularly soft iron and low-carbon steels, and is not exhibited by non-ferrous metals such as copper or brass. In practice, the points A, B, and C are very close together, and in commercial tests on mild steel the yield point, which is clearly defined, is taken to represent the elastic and proportional limits as well. After yielding, the specimen offers further resistance to deformation, although not as great as before, and further extension causes the load to rise until the point D is reached. This point marks the end of uniform extension over the whole length of the specimen, and a local extension, accompanied by a narrowing or 'necking' of the section, begins at some point along its length. This reduction in

---

*Plasticity is the ability to retain a deformation after the load producing it has been removed. In fact, it is the opposite of elasticity.

cross-sectional area causes the load to fall even though the actual stress is still rising, and the breaking load at E is in fact less than that at D. The load at D is called the *ultimate* load, since it is the maximum, and the corresponding stress is called the *ultimate tensile stress*, or *tensile strength* of the material.

Some clarification of the term 'stress' is required at this point. Normally, the stress, as defined by Eq. 3.1, is based on the original cross-sectional area, which is assumed to remain unchanged. In fact, as the specimen extends, its cross-section reduces, so that the actual stress is higher than the nominal value, which is defined thus:

$$\text{nominal stress} = \text{load}/original \text{ c.s.a.} \qquad (3.6)$$

However, until the ultimate load is exceeded, the difference between the actual and nominal stresses is negligible; this is indicated by the dotted line in Fig. 3.6. The important values of the ultimate tensile stress and the yield stress are always based on the original cross-sectional area, and are calculated by means of Eq. 3.6. Note also that, since nominal stress is proportional to load and strain is proportional to extension, the load–extension graph may be converted to a nominal stress–strain graph simply by multiplying the scales used by an appropriate factor.

To determine Young's modulus, E, from the load–extension diagram, Eq. 3.5 may be rearranged as follows:

$$E = \frac{FL}{xA} = \frac{\text{load}}{\text{extension}} \times \frac{L}{A} = \text{slope of OA} \times \frac{L}{A} \qquad (3.7)$$

In addition,

$$\text{ultimate tensile stress} = \frac{\text{ultimate load}}{\text{original c.s.a.}} \qquad (3.8)$$

and

$$\text{yield stress} = \frac{\text{load at yield point}}{\text{original c.s.a.}} \qquad (3.9)$$

For materials with no clearly defined yield point, some substitute for yield stress must be provided. This is done by finding the load corresponding to a given non-proportional extension, usually expressed as a percentage. This is called the *proof load* and the corresponding stress is the *proof stress*. A typical load–extension diagram for a non-ferrous metal is shown in Fig. 3.7, which also makes clear the method of determining the 0.1% proof load.

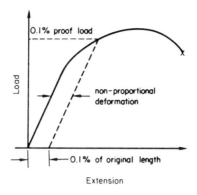

Figure 3.7

Consideration of the total extension of the specimen at fracture in relation to the orignal gauge length is a good criterion of the ductility of the material. This is its ability to be drawn out, and is important in forming processes; it also may be obtained from the load–extension diagram.

$$\text{percentage elongation at fracture} = \frac{\text{final extension}}{\text{original length}} \times 100\%$$

$$(3.10)$$

Another guide to the ductility of the material is obtained by considering reduction in cross-sectional area at the point of fracture. This, of course, must be obtained from the fractured specimen itself.

percentage reduction in area

$$= \frac{\text{original c.s.a.} - \text{c.s.a. at fracture}}{\text{original c.s.a.}} \times 100\% \qquad (3.11)$$

3.5 Factor of safety

The designer of a machine component or structural member will seek to ensure not only that it will not fracture under the applied loads but also that no permanent change in its dimensions takes place. To attain the latter object, the stress in the component must never be allowed to exceed the elastic limit stress for the material. Furthermore, since the value of the stress in the member must be calculated by using Hooke's law, the stress at the limit of proportionality should not be exceeded, as such calculations must otherwise be inaccurate.

Because of the greater precision being achieved in the calculation and prediction of stresses in engineering components, the practice of basing design, for ductile materials, on the yield point or proof stress has become more common in recent times. However, because it can be determined with greater accuracy, it is traditionally correct to use the ultimate tensile stress as the basis for design. A *factor of safety* is therefore defined, which enables a safe working stress to be calculated:

$$\text{factor of safety} = \frac{\text{ultimate tensile stress}}{\text{safe working stress}} \qquad (3.12)$$

The factor of safety used in any particular case will depend on the circumstances. For steel, factors of safety may vary from 3 for simple static loads, up to perhaps 15 for shock loads. Higher factors of safety, up to about 20, will probably be used where there are alternating stresses and a danger of metal fatigue.

The factor of safety should be chosen to ensure that the safe working stress never exceeds the stress at the limit of proportionality for the material, but, in general, other considerations will affect its value. These include:

the nature of the material, and the dependability of its specifications;

the nature of the loading, i.e., whether statically or dynamically applied or whether there is a possibility of an overload;

the likely rate of deterioration due to wear or corrosion;

the possibility of defects in manufacture;

the consequences of failure.

3.6 Shear stress

Figure 3.8(a) shows a member, fixed at one end and carrying at its free end a vertical downward load F. This force would be described as a *shearing force*, since it tends to make the material fail as in Fig. 3.8(b). Severance would occur along a plane which is parallel to the applied force, so that the portion to the right of the plane slides downwards relative to the portion to the left. Normally, shear failure will be resisted by forces of attachment along the plane and tangential to it, as shown in Fig. 3.8(c), and the presence of these internal forces constitutes a state of stress. This type of stress is called *shear stress*. The distinguishing feature of shear loading, and the resulting shear stress, is that its direction is *parallel* to the cross-sectional area resisting fracture.

shear stress, $\tau = $ shear force/unit area of resistance $= F/A$

$$(3.13)$$

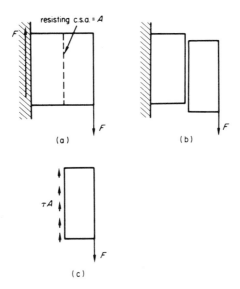

Figure 3.8

For design purposes, a maximum allowable shear stress may be calculated by using a safety factor, in the manner of Eq. 3.12, and based on the *ultimate shear stress* for the material. This, of course, must be determined by applying shear loads to a specimen of the material and testing it to destruction. As in a tensile test, the ultimate shear stress is the maximum recorded value before fracture.

Figure 3.9(a) shows a pin subjected to shear loading. To cause the pin to fail, the shearing force F must fracture it at *two* places. The pin thus has twice the area of resistance to shear, and the shear stress will be given by $\tau = F/2A$, where A is the cross-sectional area of the pin.

Such a pin is said to be in *double shear*, as opposed to the *single shear* of the rivet of Fig. 3.9(b). In theory, the strength of a pin in double shear is twice that of the same pin in single shear, but in practice this benefit is seldom achieved in full, owing to bending effects.

3.7 Shear strain

The elastic deformation produced by a shear stress may be visualized by imagining the member of Fig. 3.8(a) to consist of a large number of laminations, parallel to the shearing force F. Since each lamina carries the same load, $\tau A = F$, each lamina will slip by the

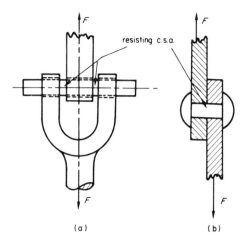

Figure 3.9

same amount relative to the adjacent lamina, and the net result is that the member will assume the shape of Fig. 3.10. The total

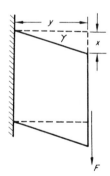

Figure 3.10

deflection due to shear at the load point is x, and this will depend on the length of the member y. A measure of the shear strain is, therefore, the shear deflection per unit length of the member.

$$\text{shear strain} = \frac{\text{deformation}}{\text{unit of original dimension}} = \frac{x}{y} = \gamma \qquad (3.14)$$

since x will, in general, be small. Thus, the measure of shear strain is the rotation of the planes perpendicular to the applied shear force.

3.8 Relation between shear stress and shear strain

Hooke's law applies equally well to shear loading as to direct loading, so that Fig. 3.3 is relevant to the problem of relating shear stress and shear strain. The main difference lies in the fact that the resistance to shear deformation is less than that due to direct loading so that the slope of the graph is smaller. Thus,

$$\text{the slope of the graph} = \frac{\text{shear stress}}{\text{shear strain}}$$
$$= \text{a constant for a given material}$$

This constant is called the *modulus of rigidity* and is denoted by G. For any given material, G must be found by means of a shear test.

$$\text{modulus of rigidity} = G = \frac{\tau}{\gamma} \qquad (3.15)$$

$$\text{i.e., } \tau = G\gamma$$

For mild steel, $G = 80 \times 10^9 \text{ N/m}^2 = 80 \text{ GN/m}^2$
For aluminium, $G = 25 \times 10^9 \text{ N/m}^2 = 25 \text{ GN/m}^2$

3.9 Physical properties of engineering materials

Certain physical properties of materials are of vital importance to the engineer, whether he be concerned with the design and operation of structural or machine components, or with production and forming processes. Means of evaluating these properties is essential so that, in any given situation, a material most appropriate to the purpose may be selected.

Some of these properties have already been referred to in the earlier sections of this chapter. The definitions of these, together with those of other properties, are summarized below.

Elasticity

This is the ability of a material to regain its original size and shape when the forces and torques producing a state of strain are removed.

Any engineering component made from a material lacking this property would be of little or no use.

Plasticity

This is the ability of a material to retain any deformation imposed on it after the removal of the forces and torques producing the state of strain.

This property is the opposite of 'elasticity' and, while it would be undesirable for any engineering component in operation, it is sometimes needed in forming processes.

Stiffness

This is defined as the force, or torque, per unit of corresponding deformation. For example, in a simple tension member the 'corresponding deformation' would be the extension produced by the tensile force, so that

$$\text{stiffness} = \frac{\text{tensile force}}{\text{extension produced}} \qquad (3.16)$$

The units of stiffness, in this case, would be N/m.

The stiffness of a spring is often referred to as 'spring rate'. Thus, if a spring extends 15 mm when a force of 45 N is applied to it,

$$\text{spring rate} = \frac{45}{15 \times 10^{-3}} = 3000 \text{ N/m} = 3 \text{ kN/m}$$

Equation 3.7 shows that Young's modulus of elasticity, E, is given by

$$E = \frac{\text{load}}{\text{extension}} \times \frac{L}{A}$$

where L and A are the length and c.s.a., respectively, of the tensile specimen. Therefore,

$$E = \text{stiffness of the specimen} \times \frac{L}{A}$$

Thus, if the tensile specimen has dimensions conforming to British Standards (BS18: *Methods for tensile testing of metals*), the modulus of elasticity E may be regarded as a measure of the 'stiffness' of the material.

Limit of proportionality

This is the maximum stress to which a material may be subjected while still conforming to the law of direct proportion between the stress and the strain produced. Beyond this stress limit, Hooke's law no longer applies.

Elastic limit

This is the maximum stress to which a material may be subjected without imposing on it a permanent deformation. Up to this value of stress, the deformation is elastic and removal of the load results in the specimen returning to its original size and shape. Beyond this value, some plastic deformation occurs.

Ductility

This is the ability of a material to 'flow', or be drawn out, without fracture occurring. This property is very important in relation to what forming processes are possible. A ductile material may be 'cold-worked', that is, stressed beyond its elastic limit in order to change its shape permanently.

Since 'force × extension' represents work done (Chapter 4), ductility is also important in relation to the ability of the material to absorb energy before fracturing. A 'tough' material will, therefore, have good ductility as well as high tensile strength.

Brittleness

This is the inability of a material to be drawn out (stretched) without fracture occurring, and is the opposite of ductility. This, of course, is an undesirable property in a material but is sometimes unavoidable. An increase in the carbon content of steel may have the effect of increasing both its tensile strength and its hardness, but it does so at the expense of making it more brittle. A low- or medium-carbon steel having a smaller tensile strength will, nevertheless, be 'tougher' because of its greater ductility or lack of brittleness.

Figure 3.11 shows stress–strain graphs for a brittle and a ductile material.

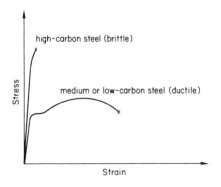

Figure 3.11

Hardness

The term 'hardness' is one with a variety of meanings; a hard material is thought of as one whose surface resists indentation or scratching, and which has the ability to indent or cut other materials. Often 'resistance to abrasion' is included in the properties mentally associated with hardness, and it may be pointed out that in fact the resistance of a material to abrasion or wear is *not* determined by its hardness; many other factors are involved. The harder of two materials may be identified by its ability to scratch the other, and a number of substances may thus be arranged in order of hardness. The 'Mohs' scale', used in classifying minerals, is a numbered list of ten minerals ranging from very hard (diamond) to very soft (talc), arranged so that each is able to scratch those listed below it, but not those listed above. Scratch tests are useful as a rough guide to the hardness of a metal—it may be compared with 'standards' of known hardness—but for the *measurement* of hardness, all tests in common use are based on *resistance to indentation*. Hardness may therefore be defined as the ability of a material to resist indentation.

In the Brinell hardness test (Fig. 3.12), a hardened steel ball (or, for very hard materials, a sintered carbide ball) is pressed into the

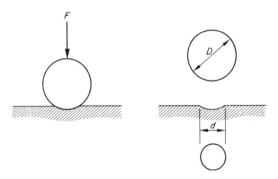

Figure 3.12

flat surface of the test piece using a specified force. The ball is then removed, and the diameter of the resulting indentation measured using a microscope. The hardness, expressed as a 'Brinell hardness number', is defined as the ratio F/A, where F is the force applied to the ball and A is the curved area of the indentation. It may be shown that

$$A = \tfrac{1}{2}\pi D[D - \sqrt{(D^2 - d^2)}]$$

where D is the diameter of the ball, and d the diameter of the indentation. The test procedure is specified by BS240: 1962, Part 1 *Testing of metals*, in which ball diameters of 1, 2, 5, and 10 mm are standardized, together with the forces to be used.

Worked examples

1. A mild-steel tie-bar is 10 mm in diameter and 2 m long. Using a factor of safety of 3, calculate the maximum load it may be permitted to carry if the ultimate tensile stress of the steel is $540 \, \text{MN/m}^2$. If $E = 200 \, \text{GN/m}^2$, what will be the extension of the tie-bar when carrying its maximum load?

From Eq. 3.12, the safe working stress $= 540/3 = 180 \, \text{MN/m}^2$
cross-sectional area $= A = \pi(0.010)^2/4 = 78.54 \times 10^{-6} \, \text{m}^2$

From Eq. 3.1, maximum safe load $= \sigma A$
$= (180 \times 10^6)(78.54 \times 10^{-6}) \, \text{N}$
$= 14\,140 \, \text{N} = 14.14 \, \text{kN}$

From Hooke's law, maximum strain $= \dfrac{\text{maximum stress}}{E}$

$$= \frac{180 \times 10^6}{200 \times 10^9} = 0.9 \times 10^{-3}$$

maximum extension $=$ maximum strain $\times$ length
$$= (0.9 \times 10^{-3}) \times 2 \, \text{m}$$
$$= 1.8 \, \text{mm}$$

2. An aluminium rod, ABC, is 1.0 m long and AB = BC. AB is 10 mm in diameter, and BC is 5 mm in diameter. The rod is subjected to a tensile load of 0.20 kN applied axially. For aluminium, $E = 70 \, \text{GN/m}^2$.
Calculate the maximum stress in the bar, and its total extension.
For a 10 mm diameter rod, the cross-sectional area
$$A = 78.54 \times 10^{-6} \, \text{m}^2$$
For a 5 mm diameter rod, the cross-sectional area
$$A = 19.64 \times 10^{-6} \, \text{m}^2$$
The maximum stress will occur in that part of the rod with the smaller diameter.

Maximum stress
$$= \sigma_{\text{BC}} = \frac{200}{19.64 \times 10^{-6}} = 10.2 \times 10^6 \, \text{N/m}^2 = 10.2 \, \text{MN/m}^2$$

From Eq. 3.5,

$$x_{AB} = \frac{200 \times 0.5}{70 \times 10^9 \times 78.54 \times 10^{-6}} = 0.182 \times 10^{-4}\,\text{m}$$

$$= 0.0182\,\text{mm}$$

$$x_{BC} = \frac{200 \times 0.5}{70 \times 10^9 \times 19.64 \times 10^{-6}} = 0.728 \times 10^{-4}\,\text{m}$$

$$= 0.0728\,\text{mm}$$

Total extension $= x_{AB} + x_{BC} = 0.0182 + 0.0728 = 0.091\,\text{mm} = 91\,\mu\text{m}$

3. A standard mild-steel tensile test specimen has a diameter of 16 mm and a gauge length of 80 mm. Such a specimen was tested to destruction, and the following results obtained:

load at yield point $= 87$ kN; extension at yield point $= 173\,\mu\text{m}$; ultimate load $= 124$ kN; total extension at fracture $= 24$ mm; diameter of specimen at fracture $= 9.8$ mm.

Calculate the modulus of elasticity of the steel, the ultimate tensile stress, the yield stress, the percentage elongation, and the percentage reduction in area.

Note that dimensions of standard tensile test specimens are given in BS18.

For a 16 mm diameter specimen, the cross-sectional area $A = 200\,\text{mm}^2$,

$$\text{yield stress} = \frac{\text{yield load}}{A} = \frac{87 \times 10^3}{200 \times 10^{-6}} = 435 \times 10^6\,\text{N/m}^2 = 435\,\text{MN/m}^2$$

Since the load at the limit of proportionality is not given, the yield stress must be used to *estimate* the value of E:

$$\text{strain at the yield point} = \frac{x}{L} = \frac{173 \times 10^{-6}}{80 \times 10^{-3}} = 2.16 \times 10^{-3}$$

$$E = \frac{\text{stress}}{\text{strain}} = \frac{435 \times 10^6}{2.16 \times 10^{-3}} = 201.4 \times 10^9\,\text{N/m}^2 = 201.4\,\text{GN/m}^2.$$

$$\text{ultimate tensile stress} = \frac{\text{ultimate load}}{A} = \frac{124 \times 10^3}{200 \times 10^{-6}} = 620 \times 10^6\,\text{N/m}^2$$

$$= 620\,\text{MN/m}^2$$

$$\text{percentage elongation} = \frac{\text{final extension at fracture}}{\text{original length, } L} \times 100\%$$

$$= \frac{24 \times 10^{-3}}{80 \times 10^{-3}} \times 100 = 30\%$$

cross-sectional area at fracture $= \pi(9.8 \times 10^{-3})^2/4 = 75.4 \times 10^{-6} \text{ m}^2$

$$\text{percentage reduction in area} = \frac{\text{reduction in area}}{A} \times 100\%$$

$$= \frac{200 - 75.4}{200} \times 100\% = 62\%$$

4. An aluminium alloy test specimen is made to standard specifications, with a diameter of 22.6 mm and a gauge length of 113 mm. A tensile test on this specimen produced the following results:

Load (kN)	0	24	48	70	96	115	124	128	133	136
Extension (mm)	0	0.09	0.17	0.25	0.34	0.44	0.55	0.68	0.90	1.11

Draw the load–extension graph, and hence deduce, for the material, the modulus of elasticity, the stress at the limit of proportionality, and the 0.1% proof stress.

The load–extension graph is plotted in Fig. 3.13.

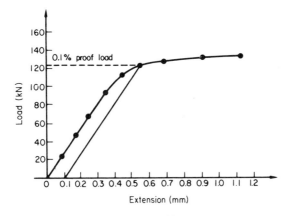

Figure 3.13

For a 22.6 mm diameter specimen, $A = 400 \text{ mm}^2$.
From Eq. 3.7,

$$E = \text{the slope of the straight-line portion} \times \frac{L}{A}$$

$$= \frac{100 \times 10^3}{0.355 \times 10^{-3}} \times \frac{113 \times 10^{-3}}{400 \times 10^{-6}} \text{ N/m}^2$$

$$= 79.6 \times 10^9 \text{ N/m}^2 = 79.6 \text{ GN/m}^2$$

The load at the limit of proportionality $= 100$ kN

$$\text{proportional limit stress} = \frac{100 \times 10^3}{400 \times 10^{-6}} \text{ N/m}^2 = 250 \text{ MN/m}^2$$

Extension corresponding to 0.1% strain $= 113 \times 0.1/100 = 0.113$ mm

The load, corresponding to a non-proportional extension of this amount, may be found by drawing a line parallel to the straight-line portion of the graph and displaced 0.113 mm from it, as shown in Fig. 3.13.

From the graph, 0.1% proof load $= 124$ kN

$$0.1\% \text{ proof stress} = \frac{124 \times 10^3}{400 \times 10^{-6}} \text{ N/m}^2 = 320 \text{ MN/m}^2$$

5. Calculate the force required to punch a circular hole, 50 mm in diameter, in a steel plate 5 mm thick. The ultimate shear stress of the steel is 200 MN/m².

The circular punch must shear through the material all around the edge of the hole.

$$\text{area to be sheared} = \text{circumference} \times \text{thickness} = \pi d \times t$$

$$= \pi \times 50 \times 5 = 785.4 \text{ mm}^2 = 785.4 \times 10^{-6} \text{ m}^2$$

$$\text{punching force} = \text{shear stress} \times \text{shear area}$$

$$= (200 \times 10^6) \times (785.4 \times 10^{-6}) \text{ N} = 157 \text{ kN}$$

6. A rectangular block of rubber, measuring $200 \times 300 \times 5$ mm, is rigidly fastened to a vertical wall, in the manner of Fig. 3.8(a), so that it projects a distance of 200 mm from the wall. The modulus of rigidity of the rubber is 1.04 MN/m².

Calculate the vertical deflection due to shear of the free vertical edge when a downward load of 100 N is applied to it.

Area of section resisting shear $= 300 \times 5 = 1500$ mm²

$$\text{shear stress in rubber} = \frac{100}{1500 \times 10^{-6}} \text{ N/m}^2 = \frac{1}{15} \text{ MN/m}^2$$

From Hooke's law,

$$\text{shear strain} = \frac{\tau}{G} = \frac{(1/15) \text{ MN/m}^2}{1.04 \text{ MN/m}^2} = 0.0641$$

But, if the vertical deflection is x mm,

$$\text{shear strain} = \frac{x}{200} \text{ (see Fig. 3.10)}$$

$$\frac{x}{200} = 0.0641, \text{ so that } x = 200 \times 0.0641 = 12.82 \text{ mm}$$

7. A pin-joint is to be made in the manner of Fig. 3.9. Find a suitable diameter for the steel pin, if the force F carried by the pin is 20 kN. The ultimate shear stress for the steel is 200 MN/m², and a factor of safety of 4 is to be used.

$$\text{Safe working stress} = \frac{200}{4} = 50 \text{ MN/m}^2$$

With reference to Fig. 3.9, the pin is in double shear, so that, if A is the cross-sectional area of the pin, the area resisting shear is $2A$. Thus,

$$\text{safe load} = 2A \times \text{safe working stress}$$
$$20 \times 10^3 = 2A \times 50 \times 10^6$$
$$A = 200 \times 10^{-6} \text{ m}^2 = 200 \text{ mm}^2$$

A 16 mm diameter rod has a sectional area of 200 mm², so that

$$\text{suitable diameter for the pin} = 16 \text{ mm}$$

Problems

1. A 14 mm diameter steel rod carries a load of 3.08 kN in tension. Calculate the stress in the material. If the rod is 2.5 m long and the modulus of elasticity is 200 GN/m², by how much will it extend?
(*Answer.* 20 MN/m², 0.25 mm.)

2. A brass rod measures 10 mm in diameter and 150 mm in length. The rod extends 0.3 mm when subjected to a tensile load. Given that for the brass, $E = 85$ GN/m², calculate the stress in the material and the magnitude of the load.
(*Answer.* 170 MN/m², 13.36 kN.)

3. A cast-iron column, 3 m long, is in the form of a tube of 200 mm external diameter and 150 mm internal diameter. The lower end is firmly based on a horizontal floor, which may be assumed rigid, and its upper end is used to support a mass of 1 tonne against the pull of gravity. If $g = 9.81$ m/s², calculate the stress induced in the tube.
Under this load, the tube is observed to contract by 17.3 μm. Determine Young's modulus for cast iron.
(*Answer.* 714 kN/m², 124 GN/m².)

4. A copper rod is 0.25 m long, and is 30 mm diameter for 150 mm of its length and 20 mm diameter for the remainder. A

tensile load is applied to the rod so that the maximum stress induced in the material is $50 \, \text{MN/m}^2$.

Determine the magnitude of the load, and calculate the total extension of the rod. For copper, $E = 103 \, \text{GN/m}^2$.

(*Answer.* 15.7 kN, 81 μm.)

5. A tie-bar is to carry a maximum load of 10 kN and is to be made from a mild steel with an ultimate tensile stress of $700 \, \text{MN/m}^2$. If a factor of safety of 3 is specified, what is the minimum diameter of bar, to the nearest millimetre, which may be used?

Determine the percentage strain in the material when a bar of this diameter carries the maximum load. For steel, $E = 200 \, \text{GN/m}^2$.

(*Answer.* 8 mm, 0.1%.)

6. A light-alloy specimen has a diameter of 16 mm and a gauge length of 80 mm. When tested in tension, the load–extension graph proved linear up to a load of 6 kN, at which point the extension was 0.034 mm.

Determine the limit of proportionality stress and the modulus of elasticity for the material.

(*Answer.* 30 MN/m², 70.5 GN/m².)

7. A specimen of mild steel, with a diameter of 20 mm and a gauge length of 100 mm, is tested to destruction and the following readings obtained:

Load (kN)	Ext. (mm)	Load (kN)	Ext. (mm)	Load (kN)	Ext. (mm)	Load (kN)	Ext. (mm)
30	0.045	124	0.195	143	0.450	198	15.8
58	0.090	132	0.210	142	0.900	204	20.0
80	0.125	138	0.225	154	4.0	199	24.6
110	0.175	141	0.240	179	9.7	185	28.0

The breaking load was 160 kN and the final elongation 31.0 mm. The diameter at the point of fracture after testing was 12.6 mm. Plot load-extension graphs, using different scales for the elastic and plastic ranges, and hence estimate: (a) Young's modulus; (b) the stress at the limit of proportionality; (c) the yield stress; (d) the ultimate tensile stress; (e) the percentage elongation; (f) the percentage reduction in area.

(*Answer.* (a) 208 GN/m² (b) 398 MN/m² (c) 455 MN/m² (d) 650 MN/m² (e) 31% (f) 60.3%.)

8. The following results were obtained from a tensile test on an aluminium alloy specimen, whose diameter was 8 mm and whose gauge length was 40 mm.

Load (kN)	0	4	6	9	12	14	15	16	17	17.4
Extension (mm)	0	0.036	0.054	0.08	0.108	0.128	0.148	0.18	0.232	0.280

Plot a graph of load against extension and use it to estimate Young's modulus and the 0.2% proof stress for the material.
(*Answer.* 90 GN/m^2, 340 MN/m^2.)

9. The compressive stress in a circular punch of 50 mm diameter is not to exceed 40 MN/m^2. What is the maximum thickness of steel plate in which a hole may be punched if the ultimate shear stress of the material is 200 MN/m^2?
(*Answer.* 2.5 mm.)

10. Explain the meaning of the term 'double shear' and, in particular, state what advantage is to be gained by adopting such an arrangement. A bolt is 25 mm in diameter and is made from mild steel with an ultimate shear stress of 200 MN/m^2. Using a factor of safety of 4, calculate the maximum safe load which the bolt can carry in double shear.
(*Answer.* 49.1 kN.)

11. A short cantilever beam is 0.5 m long and 0.25 m deep, and carries a load of 100 kN at its free end, in the manner of Fig. 3.8(a). The width of the section, which is rectangular, is 50 mm, and the material is mild steel for which G = 80 GN/m^2.

Assuming the shear stress in the material is uniformly distributed, and neglecting deformation due to other causes, calculate the deflection of the load due to shear.
(*Answer.* 0.05 mm.)

12. A coupling between two shafts is made by bolting together the flanged ends of the shafts. Six 20 mm diameter bolts are used, equally spaced around a pitch circle of 150 mm diameter. The ultimate shear stress of the material of the bolts is 240 MN/m^2, and safety factor of 4 is specified.

Calculate the maximum torque which may be transmitted through the coupling.
(*Answer.* 8.48 kN m.)

4. Work, power, and energy

4.1 Energy transferred by a force

Work is said to be done by a force when its point of application moves in the direction of its line of action. An alternative statement would be that when this happens there is a *transfer of energy*. Consider, for example, an electric hoist which is raising an object against the force of gravity. The upward force exerted on the object would be said to do work on it as the lifting proceeded. What is in fact happening is that as the object is raised it gains 'potential energy' (which will be described in Section 4.7) and this energy will (neglecting frictional and other 'losses') be equal to the electrical energy supplied to the hoist. Thus a transfer of energy is taking place and 'work' is the way in which energy is being transferred to the object being lifted.

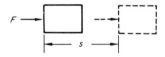

Figure 4.1

For a constant force F whose point of application moves a distance s in the direction of its line of action, as in Fig. 4.1, the amount of work done (or, the amount of energy transferred) is measured by the product of force and displacement, that is,

$$\text{work done or energy transferred} = Fs \qquad (4.1)$$

The unit of work is thus defined as the work done when unit force (1 newton) has unit displacement (1 metre); this unit is called the joule (J). Work is a form of energy transfer and, although defined with reference to work, the joule is the unit of all forms of energy, including electrical energy and heat.

It should be noted that the displacement s must be measured in

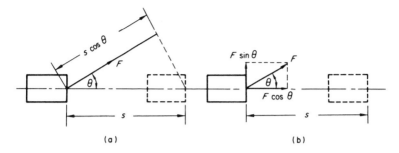

Figure 4.2

the direction in which the force F acts. If the displacement is perpendicular to the direction of the force, no work is done. A railway truck being pulled along a level track, for example, is acted on by two kinds of force: (a) an upward force which supports its weight, and (b) the horizontal force necessary to overcome friction. Only force (b) does work on the truck. If, as in Fig. 4.2, the motion of a body is at an angle to the direction of the force acting on it, the work done may be calculated in either of two ways. The displacement of the body in the direction of the force may be found, as in Fig. 4.2(a), when

$$\text{work done} = F(s \cos \theta)$$

Alternatively, the force may be resolved into two components at right angles as in Fig. 4.2(b). The component of force perpendicular to the motion, $F \sin \theta$, will do no work; hence,

$$\text{work done} = (F \cos \theta)s$$

4.2 Energy transferred by a variable force

In practice, calculations are often concerned with forces which vary during the motion of their points of application. A force which stretches a spring, for example, increases uniformly as the spring extends; and the force on a press tool varies in an irregular manner during its stroke. The way in which a force varies may be shown by a force–displacement diagram such as Fig. 4.3. In order to find the work done, the motion may be imagined to be divided into a number of parts, for example A–B in Fig. 4.3. If A and B are very close together, the force acting during this part of the motion may be considered constant and if this force is F, and the correspondinng displacement δs,

$$\text{work done between A and B} = F\delta s$$

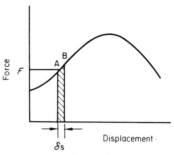

Figure 4.3

But $F\delta s$ is the area of the small vertical strip of the diagram between points A and B. The whole of the motion may be thought of as a series of very small displacements such as the one considered, and for each of these the work done will be represented by the corresponding vertical strip of the diagram. Thus the total area under the force–displacement diagram represents the total work done.

In many cases the force–displacement diagram is a simple geometrical shape (such as a triangle or trapezium) so that its area may be calculated. If the relationship between force and displacement is an irregular one, it will be necessary to construct the diagram accurately, to measure its area, and to multiply this area by the scales of force and displacement in order to obtain the work done. Areas may be found by using a planimeter, by counting squares, or by the 'mid-ordinate method' in which the diagram is divided into a number of vertical strips of equal width, and a 'mid-ordinate' is drawn at the centre of each strip. The area of each strip is, approximately, the product of its width and the length of its midordinate, hence, since all strips are of equal width,

total area = width of one strip × sum of mid-ordinates

4.3 Power

Power is defined as the *rate of energy transfer*. If this transfer is in the form of work, and is occurring at a steady rate,

power = work done/time taken

The unit of power is the watt (W), which is defined as a rate of energy transfer of 1 joule per second. This may, as above, refer to a rate of work transfer but the watt is also the unit of electrical power and of rate of heat transfer.

If a moving body has applied to it a constant force F acting in the direction of its motion, then, for a small displacement δs, from Eq. 4.1,

$$\text{work done} = F\delta s$$

If this takes place in time δt,

$$\text{power} = \text{work done/time taken}$$
$$= F\delta s/\delta t$$

But $\delta s/\delta t$ is the average velocity of the body. If δs and δt are made infinitely small,

$$\text{power} = F\,\mathrm{d}s/\mathrm{d}t = Fv \qquad (4.2)$$

where v is the instantaneous velocity of the body.

Equation 4.2 gives the constant power input to a body moving with uniform velocity or the instantaneous power in the case of a body whose velocity varies.

Worked examples

1. The force required to move a planer table against the combined resistance of cutting force and friction is 2 kN, and this force remains constant during the cutting stroke of 3 m. Find: (a) the work done; (b) the power required if the table moves at a steady speed and the stroke is completed in 5 s.

(a) From Eq. 4.1,

$$\text{work done} = Fs$$
$$= 2000 \times 3$$
$$= 6000 \text{ J or } 6 \text{ kJ}$$

(b)

$$\text{Power} = \text{work done/time taken}$$
$$= 6000/5$$
$$= 1200 \text{ W or } 1.2 \text{ kW}$$

2. A barge is towed along a canal by a rope which is inclined at 27° to the direction of motion of the barge. If a steady pull of 400 N is applied to the rope, how much work is done in towing the barge a distance of 1 km?

4. WORK, POWER, AND ENERGY

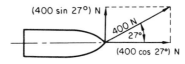

Figure 4.4

Resolving the force applied to the barge (Fig. 4.4), we have

component of force in direction of motion

$$= 400 \cos 27°$$
$$= 400 \times 0.8910$$
$$= 356.4 \text{ N}$$

Therefore,

$$\text{work done} = 356.4 \times 1000$$
$$= 356\ 400 \text{ J or } 356.4 \text{ kJ}$$

3. A spring has a free length of 200 mm and its stiffness is 12 N/mm. What is the work done in stretching the spring: (a) from 200 mm to 230 mm; (b) from 250 mm to 280 mm?

(a) The force varies uniformly from zero to $(230 - 200) \times 12 = 360$ N.

Figure 4.5(a) shows the force–displacement diagram, and

work done = area under force–displacement diagram

$$= \tfrac{1}{2} \times 0.03 \times 360 = 5.4 \text{ J}$$

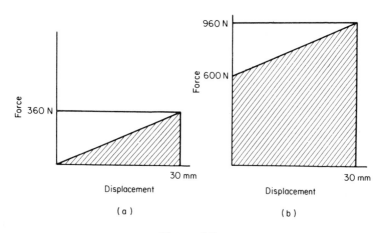

(a) (b)

Figure 4.5

(b) Initial force on spring $= (250-200) \times 12 = 600$ N

Final force on spring $= (280-200) \times 12 = 960$ N

Figure 4.5(b) shows the force–displacement diagram, and

work done $=$ area under force–displacement diagram

$$= 0.03 \times (600 + 960)/2 = 23.4 \text{ J}$$

4. A train has a mass of 200 tonnes and travels along a level track. If the frictional resistance to motion is 18 kN, find: (a) the power developed by the locomotive when it is travelling at a steady speed of 75 km/h; (b) the instantaneous power developed when it is accelerating at 0.5 m/s^2 and its instantaneous speed is 15 km/h.

(a) From Eq. 4.2,

$$\text{power} = Fv$$
$$75 \text{ km/h} = 75 \times 10^3/(60 \times 60) \text{ m/s}$$

Therefore,

$$\text{power} = 18 \times 10^3 \times 75 \times 10^3/(60 \times 60)$$
$$= 375 \times 10^3 \text{ W or } 375 \text{ kW}$$

(b) From Newton's second law, the force required to accelerate the train,

$$F = ma$$
$$= 200 \times 10^3 \times 0.5$$
$$= 100 \times 10^3 \text{ N or } 100 \text{ kN}$$

Therefore, total force to be exerted on train is

$$(18 + 100) = 118 \text{ kN}$$

Hence, from Eq. 4.2,

$$\text{power} = 118 \times 10^3 \times 15 \times 10^3/(60 \times 60)$$
$$= 492 \times 10^3 \text{ W or } 492 \text{ kW}$$

4.4 Energy transferred by a torque

Figure 4.6 shows a crank which rotates about a fixed centre O, and is acted on by a force F at a point P, distant r from O. The line of action of F is always perpendicular to OP so that its moment about O is constant; in other words, a constant torque $T = F \times r$ is applied to the shaft to which the crank is connected. Let the crank move through an angle θ (measured in radians) so that P moves to P$'$.

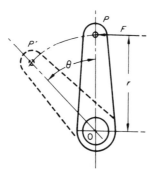

Figure 4.6

From Eq. 4.1,

work done on crank $= F \times \text{arc } PP'$

$$= F(r\theta)$$

$$= (Fr)\theta$$

But (Fr) is the applied torque T. Therefore,

$$\text{work done} = T\theta \tag{4.3}$$

4.5 Energy transferred by a fluctuating torque

The torque applied to a shaft may be constant, as in the case of the output shaft of an electric motor or a steam turbine, or it may fluctuate, as in the case of the crankshaft of a reciprocating engine. It has been shown in Section 4.2 that the work done by a variable force may be found by drawing a force–displacement diagram and measuring its area; the work done by a variable torque may be found in a similiar way.

If a torque with an instantansous value T acts over a very small angular displacement $\delta\theta$, it follows from Eq. 4.3 that

$$\text{work done} = T\delta\theta$$

This is the area of a small vertical strip of a diagram in which instantaneous values of torque are plotted vertically and angular displacements horizontally. Since the motion as a whole may be considered as a series of small angular displacements it follows that the work done by a variable torque is represented by the area of the corresponding torque-angular displacement diagram.

4.6 Power transmitted by a torque

If the torque applied to a rotating shaft is T, then for a small angular displacement $\delta\theta$, from Eq. 4.3,

$$\text{work done} = T\delta\theta$$

If this takes place in time δt,

$$\text{power} = \text{work done/time taken}$$

$$= T\delta\theta/\delta t$$

If $\delta\theta$ and δt are made infinitely small, Eq. 5.6 $d\theta/dt = \omega$ applies and

$$\text{power} = T\,d\theta/dt = T\omega \qquad (4.4)$$

where ω is the angular velocity of the shaft. If both T and ω are constant, the power will also be constant; when torque or speed are varying, Eq. 4.4 gives the instantaneous power.

Worked examples

5. A nut is being turned by a spanner to which a force of 150 N is applied. The perpendicular distance between the line of action of this force and the centre of the nut is 0.4 m. Find: (a) the torque applied to the nut; (b) the work done in turning it through an angle of 30°, assuming the torque to remain constant.

(a) Torque $= 150 \times 0.4 = 60$ N m

(b) Angular displacement $= 30° = 30 \times 2\pi/360$ rad
From Eq. 4.3,

$$\text{work done} = T\theta = 60 \times 30 \times 2\pi/360$$

$$= 31.42 \text{ J}$$

6. A 'rope brake' is used to absorb the power output of an engine under test. The arrangement is as shown in Fig. 4.7. A rope of 20 mm diameter is wrapped once round a drum of diameter 1.5 m, its upper end attached to a spring balance, and a suitable mass attached to its lower end. Find the power output of the engine when its speed is 300 rev/min, the mass attached to the rope being 40 kg, and the spring balance reading 25 N. Take $g = 9.81 \text{ m/s}^2$ and assume that the tension in the rope acts along its centre line.

$$\text{Force on 40 kg mass due to gravity} = mg = 40 \times 9.81$$

$$= 392.4 \text{ N}$$

This force is balanced by the tension in the rope, which is assumed

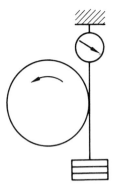

Figure 4.7

to act at its centre. Hence the clockwise torque on the drum due to this tension is

$$392.4 \times (0.75 + 0.01) \text{ N m}$$

Similarly, anticlockwise torque due to spring balance is

$$25 \times (0.75 + 0.01) \text{ N m}$$

Therefore,

net torque acting on drum $= (392.4 - 25)(0.75 + 0.01)$

$$= 367.4 \times 0.76 = 279.3 \text{ N m}$$

From Eq. 4.4,

power $= T\omega$

$$= 279.3 \times 300 \times 2\pi/60$$

$$= 8.77 \times 10^3 \text{ W or } 8.77 \text{ kW}$$

7. The end of a 120 mm diameter bar is being faced in a lathe. The bar is rotated at 100 rev/min and the tool is fed radially inwards at a steady rate. If the cutting force is 1 kN and remains constant, find: (a) the instantaneous power absorbed at the start of the operation; (b) the total work done if it is completed in 120 revolutions.

(a) At the start of the operation,

$$T = 1000 \times 0.06 = 60 \text{ N m}$$

From Eq. 4.4,

instantaneous power $= T\omega = 60 \times 100 \times 2\pi/60$

$$= 628 \text{ W}$$

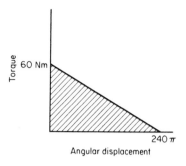

Figure 4.8

(b) The cutting force is constant, but the radius at which it acts decreases steadily. Hence, the torque-angular displacement diagram is a triangle (Fig. 4.8) and

work done = area of torque–angular displacement diagram
$$= \tfrac{1}{2} \times 120 \times 2\pi \times 60$$
$$= 22\,620 \text{ J or } 22.62 \text{ kJ}$$

4.7 Potential and kinetic energy

Energy is defined as *the capacity to do work* and, in all its forms, the unit of energy is the joule.

Potential energy is the energy possessed by a body because of its position in a gravitational field, i.e., because of its height above the ground (or any convenient datum level.) Consider (Fig. 4.9) a body of mass m at a height h above the ground. The force exerted on the body by gravity is mg, and if it is lowered to the ground gravity will do work on it; from Eq. 4.1, the amount of work done will be mgh. In other words, the position of the body relative to the ground gives it the capacity to do mgh joules of work, or

$$\text{potential energy} = mgh \qquad (4.5)$$

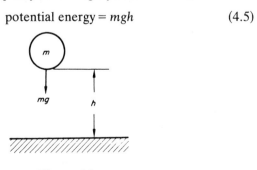

Figure 4.9

4. WORK, POWER, AND ENERGY

Kinetic energy is the energy a body possesses due to motion. From Newton's first law, it follows that a moving body can only be brought to rest by an opposing force, and while being brought to rest it will do work in overcoming this force. The amount of work the body is capable of doing before coming to rest is its kinetic energy.

Consider a body of mass m moving with velocity v, and let it be uniformly decelerated to rest in time t,

$$\text{deceleration} = v/t$$

From Newton's second law, force required

$$F = ma = mv/t$$

$$\text{distance travelled } s = \text{average velocity} \times \text{time}$$

$$= \tfrac{1}{2}vt$$

Hence, from Eq. 4.1,

$$\text{work done} = F \times s$$

$$= (mv/t) \times (\tfrac{1}{2}vt)$$

$$= \tfrac{1}{2}mv^2$$

Therefore,

$$\text{kinetic energy} = \tfrac{1}{2}mv^2 \qquad (4.6)$$

4.8 Energy and power in electrical circuits

As will be seen in Section 7.1, if the potential difference across a circuit is 1 volt then 1 joule of energy is required to cause 1 coulomb (that is, 1 ampere-second) of charge to flow round the circuit, thus:

$$\text{energy consumed by circuit} = VIt \qquad (4.7)$$

and

$$\text{power consumed} = \frac{VIt}{t} = VI \qquad (4.8)$$

In other words, the electrical power consumed, either by a complete circuit or by a single component, is the product of the potential difference across the circuit or component and the current flowing through it. A useful alternative expression may be found;

98

from Eq. 7.3, $V = IR$, where R is resistance; thus

$$\text{power consumed} = VI$$
$$= IR \times I$$
$$= I^2 R \qquad (4.9)$$

4.9 Conservation of energy

The 'principle of conservation of energy' is that *energy can neither be created nor destroyed*. Energy exists in many forms, and can be converted from one form to another, but it is found that in all such conversions the total amount of energy remains constant. It is, of course, necessary to account for *all* forms of energy when applying this principle. Energy is often said to be 'lost' – for example, by friction in a machine, or when two bodies collide – but this does not mean that it has been destroyed; only that it has been converted into an unwanted form (usually heat).

Many situations arise in which the potential energy of a body is converted into kinetic energy – for example, when a body is allowed to fall freely – and vice versa. Provided that there is no conversion of energy to heat by friction, and that the body does not receive energy, by, say, having work done on it by an external force, the principle of conservation of energy means that potential energy + kinetic energy = constant. If friction is present, the energy of the body will be reduced by the work done in overcoming frictional resistances and initial total energy = final total energy + work done against friction.

Worked examples

8. An electric hoist raises a load of mass 150 kg through a height of 10 m in 30 s. Neglecting frictional and other losses, what is the power required?

From Eq. 4.5,

$$\text{gain in potential energy} = mgh$$
$$= 150 \times 9.81 \times 10$$
$$= 14\,715 \text{ J}$$
$$\text{Power} = \text{rate of energy transfer} = \frac{\text{energy transferred}}{\text{time taken}}$$
$$= \frac{14\,715}{30}$$
$$= 490.5 \text{ W}$$

9. A vehicle of mass 5 tonnes accelerates from rest for 25 s, at the end of which time its velocity is 20 m/s. Neglecting friction, find the average power output of its engine.

From Eq. 4.6,

$$\text{final kinetic energy} = \tfrac{1}{2}mv^2$$
$$= \tfrac{1}{2} \times 5000 \times 20^2$$
$$= 10^6 \text{ J}$$

Since original kinetic energy is zero, this represents the energy to be transferred to the vehicle, hence

$$\text{power} = \text{rate of energy transfer} = \frac{\text{energy transferred}}{\text{time taken}}$$
$$= \frac{10^6}{25}$$
$$= 40 \times 10^3 \text{ W or 40 kW}$$

10. A d.c. electric motor running at 1000 rev/min is supplied at 500 V and takes a current of 15 A. What is its power input and (neglecting losses) what will be its output torque?

From Eq. 4.8,

$$\text{power input} = VI$$
$$= 500 \times 15$$
$$= 7500 \text{ W or 7.5 kW}$$

Neglecting losses, this will be the power input.
From Eq. 4.4,

$$\text{power} = T\omega$$
$$7500 = T \times 1000 \times \frac{2\pi}{60}$$
$$T = \frac{7500 \times 60}{1000 \times 2\pi}$$
$$= 71.6 \text{ N m}$$

11. A current of 5 A passes through a 20 Ω resistor. What is the power consumed and what will be the heat transfer from the resistor per minute?

From Eq. 4.9,

$$\text{power} = I^2 R$$
$$= 5^2 \times 20$$
$$= 500 \text{ W}$$

In a resistor, electrical energy is converted into heat, hence rate of heat transfer is 500 W.

$$\text{Total energy transfer} = \text{rate of transfer} \times \text{time}$$
$$= 500 \times 60$$
$$= 30\,000 \text{ J or } 30 \text{ kJ per minute}$$

12. A body of mass 5 kg is projected vertically upwards with initial velocity 20 m/s. What is its initial kinetic energy, and to what height will it rise?

From Eq. 4.6,

$$\text{kinetic energy} = \tfrac{1}{2}mv^2$$
$$= \tfrac{1}{2} \times 5 \times 20^2$$
$$= 1000 \text{ J or } 1 \text{ kJ}$$

At maximum height, the body will have zero velocity and hence zero kinetic energy. All its initial kinetic energy will have been converted to potential energy. From Eq. 4.5,

$$\text{potential energy} = mgh$$

Hence, at maximum height,

$$1000 = 5 \times 9.81 \times h$$

Therefore,

$$h = 1000/(5 \times 9.81) = 20.4 \text{ m}$$

13. In a drop-forging operation, the top die and its holder, with a combined mass of 20 kg, fall freely for 3 m before contacting the metal resting on the bottom die. Calculate: (a) the velocity of the top die at the moment of contact; and (b) the force exerted on the metal (assuming it to be constant) if the top die travels a further distance of 15 mm before coming to rest.

(a) Potential energy lost = kinetic energy gained

$$mgh = \tfrac{1}{2}mv^2$$

Therefore, $\qquad v = \sqrt{2gh}$

$$= \sqrt{(2 \times 9.81 \times 3)}$$

$$= 7.67 \text{ m/s}$$

(b) Potential energy lost = work done on metal

$$mgh = Fs$$

Therefore, $\qquad F = mgh/s$

$$= 20 \times 9.81 \times 3.015/0.015$$

$$= 39\,400 \text{ N or } 39.4 \text{ kN}$$

14. A railway truck has a mass of 6 tonnes and is at rest on an incline of 1 in 30. The brakes are released and the truck runs down the incline. If the frictional resistance to motion is 300 N, what will be its speed after travelling 20 m?

Potential energy lost = kinetic energy gained + work done against friction

$$mgh = \tfrac{1}{2}mv^2 + Fs$$

$$6000 \times 9.81 \times (20/30) = \tfrac{1}{2} \times 6000v^2 + 300 \times 20$$

$$39\,240 = 3000v^2 + 6000$$

Therefore, $\qquad v^2 = 33\,240/3000 = 11.08$

and so, $\qquad v = 3.33 \text{ m/s}$

15. A train of mass 250 tonnes starts from rest and accelerates up an incline of 1 in 100, attaining a speed of 45 km/h after travelling 250 m. The frictional resistance to motion is 30 kN. Find the work done by the locomotive and its tractive effort, assuming this to be constant.

$$45 \text{ km/h} = 45\,000/3600 = 12.5 \text{ m/s}$$

Work done on train

= increase in potential and kinetic energies + work done
against friction

$= mgh + \frac{1}{2}mv^2 + Fs$

$= 250\,000 \times 9.81 \times 250/100 + \frac{1}{2} \times 250\,000 \times 12.5^2$
$\quad + 30\,000 \times 250$

$= 6.13 \times 10^6 + 19.53 \times 10^6 + 7.5 \times 10^6$

$= 33.16 \times 10^6$ J or 33.16 MJ

work done = tractive effort × distance travelled

$33.16 \times 10^6 = F \times 250$

Therefore, $\qquad F = 33.16 \times 10^6 / 250$

$\qquad\qquad\qquad = 132.6 \times 10^3$ N or 132.6 kN

Problems

Take the acceleration due to gravity, $g = 9.81$ m/s^2.

1. A casting of mass of 30 kg is dragged 5 m along a rough
horizontal floor ($\mu = 0.4$). Find: (a) the work done; (b) the average
power absorbed if the time taken is 9 s.

(*Answer.* (a) 588.6 J (b) 65.4 W.)

2. A vehicle is towed along a level road by a rope which is
inclined at 30° to the horizontal and in which the tension is 150 N.
Find the work done in moving the vehicle 100 m.

(*Answer.* 12.99 kJ.)

3. The combined mass of a lift and its contents is 600 kg. Its
supporting cable passes over a driving pulley and is attached to a
counterweight of mass 500 kg.

Commencing from a point at which the lengths of cable on either
side of the driving pulley are equal, the lift is raised 12 m. Calculate
the work done if the mass of 1 m of cable is 3 kg.

(*Answer.* 7.54 kJ.)

4. A truck, initially at rest, is pulled along a track by a force F
which varies with its displacement s as shown in the following table:

F (N)	500	490	470	440	400	350	290
s (m)	0	5	10	15	20	25	30

Draw, to scale, a force–displacement diagram and find the work done on the truck in moving it 30 m from rest.

(*Answer.* 12.75 kJ.)

5. An electric motor runs at 1450 rev/min. Assuming its efficiency to be 80%, calculate its output torque when its power consumption is 2 kW.

(*Answer.* 10.5 N m.)

6. A 100 mm diameter bar is being turned in a lathe. The speed of the lathe is 110 rev/min and the force on the cutting tool is 1.5 kN. Calculate the power absorbed.

(*Answer.* 864 W.)

7. The torque required to drive a machine varies over one complete revolution as follows. For the first 100 degrees the torque is 50 N m and remains constant. The torque then increases uniformly over 100 degrees to a maximum of 350 N m, then decreases uniformly over 160 degrees to 50 N m. Draw a torque–angular displacement diagram and find the work done for one revolution.

(*Answer.* 995 J.)

8. A motor vehicle of mass 600 kg is travelling at 100 km/h when its brakes are applied, reducing its speed to 20 km/h. By how much is its kinetic energy reduced? What becomes of this energy?

(*Answer.* 222 kJ.)

9. A hydro-electric power station is 140 m below the level of its reservoir. If the overall efficiency of its plant is 60%, what will be the electrical power output when water flows to it from the reservoir at a rate of 30 m³/s? The density of water is 1000 kg/m³.

(*Answer.* 24.7 MW.)

10. A vehicle of mass 800 kg is at rest on a road inclined at 20° to the horizontal. Its brakes are released and it runs downhill a distance of 10 m (measured along the road). If the frictional resistance to motion is 150 N, find: (a) its velocity at this point. It continues to coast along the road, which now slopes upwards at an angle of 10° to the horizontal. If the frictional resistance is, as before, 150 N, find: (b) how far it will now travel before coming to rest.

(*Answer.* (a) 7.96 m/s (b) 16.8 m.)

11. A truck of mass 10 tonnes is moving at 1 m/s when it strikes spring-loaded buffers. The initial resisting force of the buffers is

10 kN and the resisting force increases by 100 N per mm of compression. Calculate the maximum compression of the buffers.

(*Answer.* 232 mm.)

12. A mass of 80 kg is raised vertically through a distance of 15 m in 40 s. Calculate: (a) the gain in potential energy; (b) the power required.

(*Answer.* (a) 11.772 kJ (b) 294.3 W.)

13. A mass of 500 kg is accelerated from rest for 30 s, at the end of which time its velocity is 15 m/s. What is: (a) the final kinetic energy; (b) the average power expended?

(*Answer.* (a) 56.25 kJ (b) 1.875 kW.)

14. An electric traction vehicle is being decelerated by making its driving motor function as a generator, feeding energy back to the supply. If the mass of the vehicle is 10 tonnes and it decelerates from 20 m/s to 15 m/s in 12.5 s, what will be the average power output (neglecting frictional and other losses)?

(*Answer.* 2.8 kW.)

15. A d.c. motor running at 1500 rev/min is supplied at 400 V and takes a current of 7.5 A. What is its power input and (neglecting losses) what will be its output torque?

(*Answer.* 3 kW, 19.1 N m.)

16. Neglecting losses, calculate the torque required to drive the generator attached to a motor vehicle engine if it delivers a current of 25 A at 12 V when running at 1800 rev/min.

(*Answer.* 1.59 N m.)

17. A current of 4 A passes through an electric-fire element of resistance 60 Ω. What is the power consumed and how much heat energy will have been produced in 30 s?

(*Answer.* 960 W, 28.8 kJ.)

18. The conductors in a power cable have a total resistance of 0.05 Ω. What is the 'power loss' due to the cable resistance when it carries a current of 100 A?

(*Answer.* 500 W.)

19. A projectile of mass 4 kg is fired vertically upwards with initial velocity 250 m/s. Neglecting air resistance find: (a) its initial

kinetic energy; (b) its velocity when at a height of 1000 m; (c) its maximum height.

(*Answer.* (a) 125 kJ (b) 207 m/s (c) 3185 m.)

20. A train of total mass 200 tonnes starts from rest and accelerates up an incline of 1 in 80. If the locomotive exerts a steady tractive effort of 100 kN and the frictional resistance to motion is 25 kN, what will be the speed of the train after it has travelled 300 m?

(*Answer.* 12.3 m/s.)

5. Friction

5.1 The nature of friction

Very few engineering situations occur in which friction does not play some part. In some cases it is gainfully employed, as in clamping devices and friction drives. More frequently, it exists as an integral part of the situation merely because it cannot be eradicated, and it results in the dissipation of energy and the gradual erosion of material from the component involved.

This erosion of material, or wear, due to friction represents a substantial ecomonic loss to the community in general. Because of this, a considerable amount of research has been undertaken in recent years aimed at a greater understanding of the processes involved and the development of methods by which it may be reduced.

Friction, and hence wear, may be reduced by the method of lubrication, in which surfaces having relative motion are separated by a fluid film. The cheapest fluid which could be used for this purpose is water. Unfortunately, this has a corrosive effect on ferrous materials and so the second most plentiful, which is oil, is normally used.

Friction, wear, and lubrication, are thus inevitably bound together, and the study of these related topics is called 'tribology'. This subject is very large and, of necessity, this chapter must confine itself to the basic laws of dry friction or, as it is sometimes called, *coulomb friction*.

Surfaces, normally described as 'flat' or 'smooth', are in fact covered with undulations and bumps. Microscopic examination of a so-called 'flat' surface would reveal a terrain which one notable tribologist has likened to the Lake District! This comparison is a good one because it emphasizes not only the irregular surface geometry but also the surface contamination which is always present. A 'dry' surface is, by definition, one with *all* surface contamination removed – and this includes dust particles and surface film as well as any moisture. It will be appreciated from this definition that a *dry* surface is difficult, if not impossible, to achieve in practice. It is

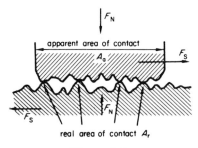

Figure 5.1

for this reason that elementary laboratory experiments designed to verify the laws of dry friction frequently prove to be unsatisfactory.

Consider two dry surfaces in contact as in Fig. 5.1. The surface irregularities are shown magnified to illustrate that the real area of contact, A_r, is considerably smaller than the apparent area of contact, A_a. Because the real area is so small, the stresses at points of contact will be very large. If the normal force, F_N, pressing the surfaces together, is increased, two things will happen: the existing points of contact will tend to flatten under the large stresses and, in consequence, further points of contact will be established, both occurrences causing the real area of contact to increase. A reasonable hypothesis is that A_r is directly proportional to F_N, so that

$$F_N = k_1 A_r \qquad (5.1)$$

where k_1 is a constant depending on the surface geometry and the properties of deformation of the materials.

Suppose now a force F_S is applied tending to cause relative sliding of the surfaces (Fig. 5.1). If sliding is to occur the force F_S must shear the points of contact, which will have welded together under the action of the very large stresses there. The force F_S required will thus be directly proportional to the area of material to be sheared, A_r, so that

$$F_S = k_2 A_r \qquad (5.2)$$

where k_2 is a constant, and will in fact be the ultimate shear stress of the material.

Dividing Eq. 5.2 by Eq. 5.1 gives:

$$\frac{F_S}{F_N} = \frac{k_2 A_r}{k_1 A_r} = \frac{k_2}{k_1} = \mu \qquad (5.3)$$

The ratio of the force necessary to produce sliding to the normal force of reaction between the surfaces is thus seen to be a constant, independent of the real area of contact since this cancels out. This constant is called the *coefficient of limiting friction* and is denoted by μ.

For extremely dry surfaces, obtainable by special high-vacuum techniques, μ can be quite large, but surface contamination which is always present under normal conditions reduces its value to less than 1.0. A typical value for two relatively smooth metal surfaces in contact is about 0.3.

By its very nature, the force due to friction is a *reaction*, in that it opposes any force tending to slide one surface relative to the other. As a reaction, it is equal and opposite to the applied force tending to produce motion, but there is a *limit* to the value it may reach. It is to this limiting value that Eq. 5.2 refers. In Fig. 5.2(a), a block resting on a fixed surface is acted on by a force P which gradually increases from zero as indicated by the graph of Fig. 5.2(b). This produces a reactionary coulomb friction force F_C which, at first, is equal and opposite to P so that no motion occurs. Eventually, however, P reaches a value beyond which F_C cannot rise, and as P continues to increase F_C remains at this limiting value. The limiting value of the force of friction is given by Eq. 5.3, which may be written in the form

$$F_C = F_S = \mu F_N \qquad (5.4)$$

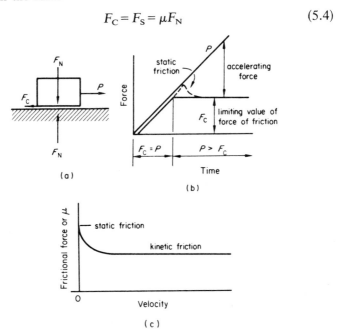

(a)

(b)

(c)

Figure 5.2

When P exceeds this value, slipping occurs. On the point of slipping, however, a slightly larger force is required to overcome friction due to the initial shearing action required to produce detachment of the surfaces. Figure 5.2(c) shows how the limiting value of the friction force, or μ, varies with the velocity. Static friction, or 'stiction' as it is sometimes colloquially called, is seen to be greater than the kinetic value, which, for dry friction remains constant as the velocity of sliding increases.

5.2 The laws of dry friction

A number of conclusions may be drawn from the foregoing discussion, and may be presented as a series of laws. These laws were first propounded by Coulomb (hence the term 'coulomb friction') and are based mainly on experimental observations. These laws are by no means exact, partly because 'dry' surfaces do not in practice occur and partly because the laws themselves tend to oversimplify the problem. Nevertheless, these laws form a useful basis for engineering calculations, and suffice for the majority of general applications.

(1) When external forces tend to cause one surface to slide over another surface, a reactionary force of friction, acting tangentially to the surfaces, is set up so as to oppose the motion.
(2) There is a limiting value of the force of friction beyond which it cannot rise. If the forces tending to produce the relative motion exceed this value, slipping begins.
(3) The force necessary to initiate relative motion is greater than that needed to maintain it. Static friction is greater than kinetic friction.
(4) The limiting value of the force of friction is quite independent of the area of contact.
(5) The limiting value of the force of kinetic friction is independent of the velocity of sliding.
(6) The limiting value of the force of friction bears a constant ratio to the normal reaction between the surfaces. This constant ratio is called the coefficient of limiting friction, and is denoted by μ.
(7) The coefficient of limiting friction is dependent on the nature of the surfaces in contact. This refers to the surface geometry, the surface contamination, and the physical properties of the materials involved.

The sixth law gives rise to Eq. 5.4, which is now restated:

$$F_C = \mu F_N$$

where F_C is the limiting value of the force of coulomb friction,
  μ is the coefficient of limiting friction,
  F_N is the normal reaction between the surfaces.

Note carefully that this equation may be applied only when there is relative sliding between the surfaces, in which case the value of μ will be that corresponding to kinetic friction. If the equation is applied when the surfaces are *on the point of slipping*, then the value of μ used should be that corresponding to static friction, and will be greater (see Fig. 5.2(c)).

5.3 The angle of friction

Figure 5.3 shows a block of mass m which is moving with constant velocity along a horizontal plane. The block is subjected to two externally applied forces, the horizontal force P, and the force due to gravity mg. The force of gravity is reacted by the normal reaction F_N, and the force P is reacted by the frictional force F_C which, because the block is moving, will be at its limiting value. Equation 5.4 thus applies, μ having its kinetic value. F_C and F_N are both reactions and may be regarded as components of a single resultant reaction R, which is the vector sum of F_C and F_N. Because of friction, this resultant reaction R is inclined backwards from the normal to the plane by an angle ϕ. This is called the *angle of friction*. With reference to the vector sum of the reactions (Fig. 5.3),

$$\tan \phi = \frac{F_C}{F_N} = \mu \qquad (5.5)$$

Since the block has constant velocity, it is in equilibrium under the action of the three forces P, mg, and the resultant reaction R. This fact is expressed by the polygon of forces, also shown in Fig. 5.3.

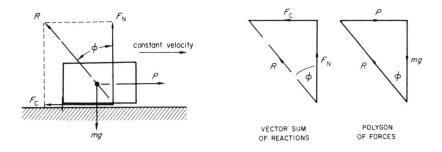

Figure 5.3

5.4 The effect of lubrication

In situations where friction is undesirable and wasteful (in terms of both energy and material), methods of reducing its effects must be sought. The obvious solution to the problem is to separate the two surfaces by means of a layer of fluid. This process is called 'lubrication', and the fluid used a 'lubricant'.

A lubricant can be either a gas (air) or a liquid (oil), the latter being the more common. To be effective, the lubricant must be pressurized sufficiently to overcome the normal pressure between the surfaces and hence produce the required separation. This pressure is sometimes artificially induced, as in hydrostatic lubrication, but more usually is generated by a natural process called hydrodynamic lubrication. These matters are complex and should, therefore, be considered at a higher level of study.

Although effective lubrication considerably reduces frictional effects, it does not eliminate them altogether. The lubricant itself possesses an internal effect, similar to friction, called 'viscosity'. Viscous forces within the fluid will tend to resist the relative motion of the surfaces it is separating, but these forces are very small compared with those due to dry friction.

Worked examples

1. A body of mass 10 kg rests on a horizontal plane. The coefficient of static friction between the contact surfaces is 0.4, and the coefficient of kinetic friction is 0.25. A gradually increasing horizontal force is applied to the body, and this eventually causes the body to slide along the plane.

Determine the force of friction acting on the body: (a) when the body is at rest; (b) when the body is on the point of slipping; (c) when the body is actually sliding.

The situation described is similar to those of Fig. 5.2(a) and Fig. 5.3.

The normal reaction will equal the force due to gravity:

$$F_N = mg = 10 \times 9.81 = 98.1 \text{ N (since } g = 9.81 \text{ m/s}^2)$$

(a) When the body is at rest, the force of friction will be equal and opposite to the applied horizontal force, at any particular instant.

This will apply until the body is on the point of slipping.

(b) When the body is on the point of slipping,

$$F_C = \mu F_N \quad \text{where} \quad \mu = 0.4$$
$$F_C = 0.4 \times 98.1 = 39.24 \text{ N}$$

(c) When sliding is taking place,

$$F_C = \mu F_N \quad \text{where} \quad \mu = 0.25$$
$$F_C = 0.25 \times 98.1 = 24.53 \text{ N}$$

2. A block of mass 10 kg is pushed along horizontal fixed guides by a force acting downwards at 30° to the horizontal, as shown in Fig. 5.4. Assuming $g = 10$ m/s^2 and that the coefficient of limiting friction is 0.3, determine the mimimum value of the force necessary to maintain constant velocity, the normal reaction between block and guides, and the magnitude of the frictional force.

$$\text{force due to gravity} = mg = 10 \times 10 = 100 \text{ N}$$

The block is in equilibrium under the action of the applied force P, the force of gravity mg, and the resultant reaction R. Since sliding is occurring, R will be inclined to the normal at the angle of friction ϕ, where $\tan \phi = 0.3$; $\phi = 16° 42'$. The polygon of forces may now be drawn to some suitable scale, as in Fig, 5.4(b), from which $R = 126.3$ N, $P = 41.9$ N. The resultant reaction R may now be resolved into its normal and tangential components F_N and F_C which, as indicated by Fig. 5.4(c), are

$$\text{normal reaction } F_N = R \cos \phi = 126.3 \cos 16° 42' = 121.0 \text{ N}$$
$$\text{frictional force } F_C = R \sin \phi = 126.3 \sin 16° 42' = 36.3 \text{ N}$$

3. With reference to the previous problem, calculate the work done against friction when the block moves a distance of 500 mm

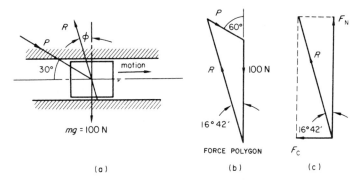

Figure 5.4

along the fixed guides. In what form will this energy expended reappear?

The work done by a force is dealt with in the previous chapter, Section 4.1.

$$\text{work done against friction} = \text{frictional force} \times \text{displacement}$$
$$= 36.3 \times 0.500 \text{ J}$$
$$= 18.15 \text{ J}$$

Energy expended in overcoming friction always reappears in the form of *heat.*

4. A simple journal bearing carries a load of 10 kN. The diameter of the bearing is 50 mm, and the shaft rotates at 3000 rev/min. If the coefficient of friction is 0.01, estimate the power absorbed by friction.

The normal reaction at the point of contact of shaft and bearing will be approximately equal to the bearing load.

$$\text{tangential force of friction} = \mu F_N = (0.01)(10\,000) = 100 \text{ N}$$
$$\text{frictional torque} = \text{force} \times \text{radius} = 100(0.025) = 2.5 \text{ N m}$$
$$\text{angular velocity of shaft} = 3000(2\pi/60) = 314.2 \text{ rad/s}$$

From Section 4.6,

$$\text{power absorbed} = T\omega = 2.5 \times 314.2 \text{ W}$$
$$= 785.4 \text{ W} = 0.785 \text{ kW}$$

This is also the rate at which heat must be removed from the bearing to prevent overheating – that is, 785.4 J of heat must be removed each second.

Problems

1. Define the term 'coefficient of limiting friction'.
A mass of 100 kg is dragged along a horizontal surface at constant velocity by means of a horizontal force of 0.2 kN. Assuming $g = 10 \text{ m/s}^2$, calculate the coefficient of limiting friction between the mass and the floor.
If the mass is dragged 5 m in this manner, what is the work done against friction?
(*Answer.* 0.2, 1.0 kJ.)

2. The coefficient of friction between the table of a planing machine and its slideways is 0.1. The cutting stroke is 1.5 m long,

and the number of cutting strokes per minute is 25. If the combined mass of the table and work-piece is 1200 kg, estimate the average power absorbed by friction. Assume $g = 10 \text{ m/s}^2$.

(*Answer.* 1.5 kW.)

3. Distinguish between static friction and kinetic friction. A mass of 50 kg is at rest on a horizontal floor. The coefficient of kinetic friction between the mass and the floor is 0.3. A force, acting upwards at 45° to the horizontal, is applied to the mass, and is gradually increased from zero. When this force reaches 200 N, the mass just begins to slide. What is the coefficient of static friction between the mass and the floor? If the force is subsequently maintained at 200 N, what will be the acceleration of the mass?

(*Answer.* 0.394, 0.676 m/s^2.)

4. A cable is attached to a casting of mass 1.5 tonne, which is then drawn a distance of 12 m at constant velocity across the foundry floor. If the coefficient of friction is 0.4 and $g = 9.81 \text{ m/s}^2$, determine the tension in the cable and the total work done if: (a) the cable is horizontal; (b) the cable is inclined at 25° to the horizontal. (1 tonne = 1000 kg.)

(*Answer.* (a) 5.89 kN, 70.6 kJ (b) 5.47 kN, 59.5 kJ.)

5. A 100 mm diameter shaft runs in a journal bearing at 1000 rev/min. The load on the bearing is 25 kN and the coefficient of friction is 0.008. If the bearing is cooled by circulating water, at the rate of 1.5 litre/min, through passages in the bearing housing, estimate the rise in temperature of the cooling water, assuming steady-state conditions. The specific heat of water is 4.2 kJ/kg °C, and the mass of 1 litre of water is 1 kg.

(*Answer.* 9.97 °C.)

6. Simple machines

6.1 The purpose of a machine

A machine is a device which enables work to be done more conveniently. In general, it has an input member to which is applied an input force or torque, known as the *effort,* and an output member which carries an output force or torque, known as the *load.* Usually, the purpose of the machine is fulfilled if, by virtue of its design, the effort required is very much smaller than the load. A properly designed lifting device, for example, enables large gravitational loads to be overcome by the application of quite small forces. A machine can thus allow a man to lift a load which otherwise he would not have the physical strength to raise.

When the output member of a machine moves the load applied to it, work is done *by* the machine on, or against, the load. This may be called the *work output.* This work output occurs only in consequence of the work done *on* the machine when the effort moves the input member. The work done on the machine by the effort may be called the *work input.* By the principle of conservation of energy (Section 4.9), it is impossible for the work output to exceed the work input. Indeed, in practice, the work output is always less than the input because some energy must be expended within the machine itself in overcoming friction which resists the relative motion of the moving parts.

An *ideal machine* is one in which there is no friction (and no inertia), so that for such a machine (Fig. 6.1):

$$\text{work input} = \text{work output}$$
$$F_i x_i = F_o x_o \tag{6.1}$$

where F_i = input force or effort, F_o = output force or load, x_i = input displacement, x_o = output displacement.

It is clear from Eq. 6.1 that if F_i is to be small while F_o is large, the reverse must be true of the corresponding displacements. Thus, to gain the advantage offered by the concept of a machine, it must be designed so that the input displacement of the effort is greater than the output displacement of the load.

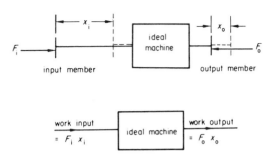

Figure 6.1

6.2 Mechanical advantage and velocity ratio

The advantage offered by a machine is that the effort can be very much smaller than the load. The measure of this advantage is the ratio of load to effort, and this is called the *mechanical advantage* (M.A.), or *force ratio*.

$$\text{Mechanical advantage} = \frac{\text{load}}{\text{effort}} = \frac{F_o}{F_i} \qquad (6.2)$$

To obtain this mechanical advantage, the machine must be designed so that the input displacement of the effort is much greater than the output displacement of the load. The measure of this is the ratio of input to output displacements, and is called the *velocity ratio* (V.R.), or *movement ratio*.

$$\text{Velocity ratio} = \frac{\text{input displacement of effort}}{\text{output displacement of load}} = \frac{x_i}{x_o} \qquad (6.3)$$

Since both displacements occur in the same time, this is also the ratio of the input and output velocities.

The V.R. of a machine is a constant, since it is entirely dependent on the physical geometry given to it by its design and manufacture. On the other hand, the M.A. of a machine varies with the load it carries. This is because, except in an ideal machine, the effort required to overcome the frictional forces within the machine compares differently with the various loads applied. With a very small load, for example, more effort may be needed to overcome the friction than the load itself, whereas, for a large load, the part of the effort used to overcome friction may be only a small percentage of the whole. The situation is further complicated by the increase in the frictional forces as the loading is increased, owing to the tendency of the load to increase the normal reactions between the contact surfaces of the moving parts.

For these reasons, the M.A. to be expected from an ideal machine is never achieved in practice. In general, however, the M.A. increases with the load and tends towards a limiting value, as will be shown in Section 6.4.

6.3 Efficiency

In practice, the useful work output of a machine is less than the work input (Fig. 6.2). The difference represents energy wasted, and this must be reduced to the smallest possible proportions by suitable design and use of the machine. The aim should be to make the useful work output as high a proportion of the work input as possible, and the measure of success achieved in this respect is called the *efficiency* of the machine,

$$\text{efficiency} = \eta = \frac{\text{work output}}{\text{work input}} = \frac{F_o x_o}{F_i x_i} \tag{6.4}$$

This is usually expressed as a percentage, in which case the ratio is multiplied by 100.

In the ideal machine, no energy is wasted and the efficiency is 1.0, or 100%, so that Eq. 6.4 reverts to Eq. 6.1. Since x_o and x_i are fixed by the geometry of the machine, the only quantity which may vary for a given load, F_o, is the input force or effort, F_i. In a real machine, the *actual effort* is always greater than the *ideal effort* because of friction in the machine. The difference between these two is called the *friction effort*.

It is possible to express the efficiency of a machine in terms of its M.A. and V.R. Equation 6.4 may be rewritten:

$$\text{efficiency} = \eta = \frac{F_o}{F_i} \times \frac{x_o}{x_i} = \frac{F_o/F_i}{x_i/x_o} = \frac{\text{M.A.}}{\text{V.R.}} \tag{6.5}$$

ince, for any given machine, the V.R. is a constant, the efficiency

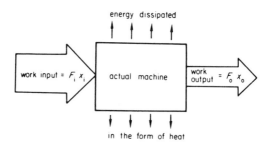

energy dissipated

work input = $F_i x_i$

actual machine

work output = $F_o x_o$

in the form of heat

Figure 6.2

must vary in the same manner as the M.A. does, so that the efficiency will increase with the load. However, the efficiency tends towards a limiting value as the load is increased, as will be shown in Section 6.4. In general, machines with high velocity ratios, such as the screw-jack, tend to have lower efficiencies than those having only moderate velocity ratios.

Note that the definition of efficiency as work output/work input is applicable over a wide field. The purpose of some machines, for example, is to convert energy from one form to another, as in a heat engine or electrical generator. Since all forms of energy have the same units, this presents no problem in calculating efficiencies.

Consider a simple machine, say a lifting device, which does work on a load, and suppose the load retains the useful work output in the form of potential energy. If this potential energy was 51 J and the work input had been 100 J, then the efficiency would be 51% and 49 J of energy would have been expended in overcoming friction. If the effort is now removed, the machine will run backwards because the 51 J of energy contained by the load is sufficient to overcome friction, since this will require only a further 49 J, leaving 2 J to spare. On the other hand, if 51 J had been required to overcome friction during the run-up, the 49 J retained by the load would be insufficient for the further expenditure of energy needed to make the machine run backwards, when the effort is removed. This reversal of a machine, which may occur on removal of the effort, is called *overhauling*. A machine having an efficiency less than 50% cannot overhaul. Machines with efficiencies greater than 50% should, therefore, be fitted with a non-reversal device – a safety ratchet, for example – to prevent them running-back.

6.4 The characteristics of a machine

For any given machine, the V.R. is fixed and may be calculated from its geometry. The actual effort, the M.A., and the efficiency of the machine, however, all vary with the load and cannot be calculated. These must therefore be determined experimentally. The graphs showing their variation with load are called the *characteristics* of the machine.

The fundamental characteristic is the variation of actual effort with load. Once this is known, the M.A. and efficiency may be deduced from it. Figure 6.3 shows a typical graph of actual effort against load for a simple machine. Since this is a straight line, its equation is of the form

$$F_i = aF_o + b \qquad (6.6)$$

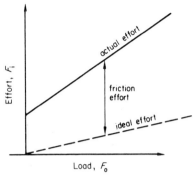

Figure 6.3

where a and b are constants. This equation is known as 'the law of the machine'. The constant b is evidently the effort required when there is zero load on the machine. For an ideal machine, this is zero so that the ideal effort is represented by a straight line passing through the origin (shown dotted in Fig. 6.3). The difference between the actual and ideal efforts is the effort required to overcome friction. This also is indicated in Fig. 6.3.

The M.A. may be deduced from the law of the machine.

$$\text{M.A.} = \frac{F_o}{F_i} = \frac{F_o}{aF_o + b} = \frac{1}{a + (b/F_o)} \tag{6.7}$$

The variation of the M.A. with load, as represented by this equation, is shown in Fig. 6.4. When F_o is very large, b/F_o becomes negligible compared with a, so that the M.A. approaches a limiting value and Eq. 6.7 reduces to:

$$\text{M.A.}_{\text{(limiting)}} = \frac{1}{a} \tag{6.8}$$

Having obtained the M.A., the efficiency is best found from Eq. 6.5.

$$\text{efficiency} = \eta = \frac{\text{M.A.}}{\text{V.R.}} = \frac{1}{\text{V.R.}[a + (b/F_o)]} \tag{6.9}$$

Since the V.R. is a constant, the variation of efficiency with load is similar to that of the M.A. (see Fig. 6.4), and it also will approach a limiting value,

$$\eta_{\text{(limiting)}} = \frac{1}{(\text{V.R.})a} \tag{6.10}$$

since b/F_o tends to zero as F_o becomes large.

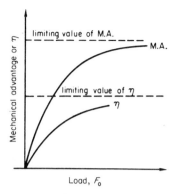

Figure 6.4

6.5 Levers

The lever is, perhaps, the simplest example of a machine. Its operation relates to the principle of moments (Section 2.7) and, by adjusting the lengths of moment arms, the ratio of load to effort (M.A.) can be varied. Three systems, or *orders*, of lever are possible, and these are shown in Fig. 6.5.

The distinguishing feature of these three systems is the position of the fulcrum, or pivot, of the lever in relation to the load, F_o, and the effort, F_i. In Fig. 6.5, the point of application of the effort, the fulcrum, and the point of attachment of the load, are labelled A, B, and C, respectively, in each case. By simple geometry, and by Eq. 6.3,

$$\text{V.R.} = \frac{x_i}{x_o} = \frac{\text{AB}}{\text{BC}} \tag{6.11}$$

for all three systems.

With reference to Fig. 6.5, it will be observed that:

for a 1st-order lever, the V.R. *can* be greater than unity;
for a 2nd-order lever, the V.R. *must* be greater than unity;
for a 3rd-order lever, the V.R. must be *less than* unity.

Although there is little or no friction involved in a lever system, 100% efficiency cannot be achieved because, in practice, some effort will be required to overcome the weight of the lever itself, even when no load is applied. However, if the weight of the lever is

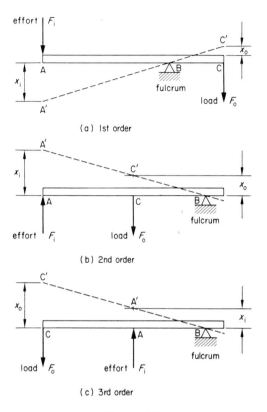

(a) 1st order

(b) 2nd order

(c) 3rd order

Figure 6.5

neglected then, by the principle of moments,

$$F_i \times AB = F_o \times BC$$

so that:

$$M.A. = \frac{F_o}{F_i} = \frac{AB}{BC} \tag{6.12}$$

Equations 6.11 and 6.12 give identical results for V.R. and M.A., which is to be expected for ideal conditions (100% efficiency). In practice, this would not be the case because of the weight of the lever.

A disadvantage of the simple lever is the limitation on the possible displacement of the load. This problem is overcome in the *wheel and axle*, which is an extension of the 1st-order simple lever principle. Figure 6.6 shows a diagram of the wheel and axle.

Let the effort F_i be given a downward displacement equivalent to

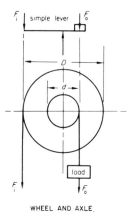

WHEEL AND AXLE

Figure 6.6

one revolution of the wheel:

$$\text{input displacement of effort} = x_i = \pi D$$

since a length of cord equal in length to the circumference of the wheel will be unwound from the wheel.

This will cause the load to be displaced upwards, as a length of cord equal to the circumference of the axle is wound on to the axle,

$$\text{output displacement of load} = x_o = \pi d$$

$$\text{velocity ratio} = \frac{x_i}{x_o} = \frac{\pi D}{\pi d} = \frac{D}{d} \tag{6.13}$$

6.6 Pulley systems

Arrangements of pulleys connected by a single rope may be used to gain a mechanical advantage in situations where heavy loads are to be lifted. Figure 6.7 shows an example of such a pulley system.

In the simple pulley-block arrangement, pulleys of equal diameter are used in two blocks, as shown, with a single rope passing over each pulley in turn. One end of the rope is fixed, either to the upper or to the lower block (whichever is convenient), while the free end is used for applying the effort. For the case illustrated, the lower block is suspended from the upper block by three sections of the rope. The rope between the blocks is shortened by whatever displacement is given to the effort, and this contraction must be shared between the three sections. The load is therefore raised by only one-third of the input displacement, and the V.R. is evidently 3. In general, the

PULLEY BLOCKS

Figure 6.7

V.R. of a set of pulley blocks is equal to the number of sections of rope by which the lower block is supported, or, alternatively, is equal to the total number of pulleys used. Thus, for a pulley-block system,

$$V.R. = \frac{\text{number of sections of rope}}{\text{supporting the lower block}} = \frac{\text{total number}}{\text{of pulleys used}} \qquad (6.14)$$

For an ideal system, the M.A. gained would also be given by Eq. 6.14 but, in practice, friction and the weight of the pulley block would reduce the value of the M.A., and the actual effort required would be greater than the ideal effort.

6.7 Gear systems

In a simple gear train, toothed wheels are used to transmit angular motion from one wheel to another. The axes of the wheels are fixed and, since the teeth on one wheel are required to engage with the teeth on the other, the teeth on all wheels must be of the same size. A consequence of this is that the number of teeth on each wheel must be proportional to its mean diameter, or *pitch circle diameter* (P.C.D.). That is,

$$\frac{T_A}{T_B} = \frac{D_A}{D_B} \qquad (6.15)$$

where T_A and T_B, respectively, are the numbers of teeth on wheels A and B, and D_A and D_B, respectively, are the P.C.D.s of wheels A and B.

Figure 6.8 shows a simple gear train involving only two wheels A

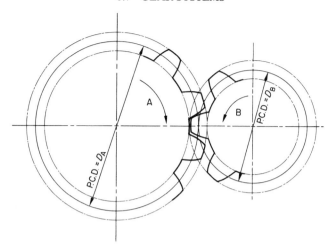

Figure 6.8

and B. Suppose A has 30 teeth and B only 10 teeth. If A were to make one complete revolution, there would be 30 engagements of mating teeth on each wheel, which would mean that B must make three complete revolutions. In other words,

$$\text{number of revs of wheel B} = \frac{30}{10} \times \text{number of revs of wheel A}$$

Or, in general,

$$\text{revs of B} = \frac{T_A}{T_B} \times \text{revs of A} \qquad (6.16)$$

Thus, a velocity ratio exists between a pair of mating gear wheels:

$$\text{V.R.} = \frac{\text{revs of B}}{\text{revs of A}} = \frac{T_A}{T_B} = \frac{D_A}{D_B} \qquad (6.17)$$

Comparison between this equation and Eq. 6.3 will show that, in terms of a simple machine, B is the wheel to which the effort torque would be applied and A is the wheel carrying the load torque.

Again, assuming 100% efficiency,

$$\text{M.A.} = \text{V.R.} = \frac{T_A}{T_B} = \frac{D_A}{D_B} \qquad (6.18)$$

but, in practice, friction would reduce the actual mechanical advantage obtained.

Figure 6.9 shows a simple gear train involving three gear wheels

125

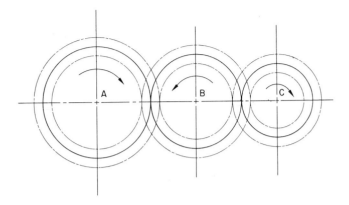

Figure 6.9

A, B, and C. It follows from Eq. 6.16 that

$$\text{revs of } C = \frac{T_B}{T_C} \times \text{revs of B}$$

$$= \frac{T_B}{T_C} \times \frac{T_A}{T_B} \times \text{revs of A}$$

$$= \frac{T_A}{T_C} \times \text{revs of A}$$

Thus, for the simple gear train of Fig. 6.9,

$$\text{V.R.} = \frac{\text{revs of } C}{\text{revs of A}} = \frac{T_A}{T_C} = \frac{D_A}{D_C} \qquad (6.19)$$

The main feature to note about Eq. 6.19 is that the velocity ratio, or gear ratio, is independent of wheel B. For this reason, wheel B is known as an *idler* wheel.

Any number of idler wheels may be used in a simple train, their only purpose being:

(1) to change the sense of rotation of the output shaft;
(2) to act as 'spacers' when the distance between centres of input and output shafts is excessive, thereby avoiding the need for very large-diameter gear wheels.

The fact that idler wheels have no effect on the overall velocity ratio places a limitation on the magnitude of ratios possible in practice.

A *compound* gear train, however, employs intermediate wheels, between input and output, which *do* affect the overall V.R., making much larger gearbox ratios a practical possibility. Compound wheels

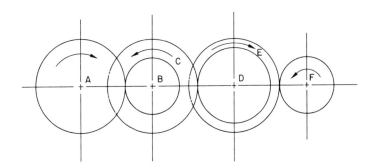

Figure 6.10

are used, these consisting of two wheels of different sizes keyed to the same shaft. One of these wheels is driven by the preceding wheel while the other drives the next wheel in the train, as shown in Fig. 6.10. With reference to Fig. 6.10, and to Eq. 6.16,

$$\text{revs of F} = \frac{T_E}{T_F} \times (\text{revs of DE})$$

$$= \frac{T_E}{T_F} \times \left(\frac{T_C}{T_D} \times \text{revs of BC} \right)$$

$$= \frac{T_E}{T_F} \times \frac{T_C}{T_D} \times \left(\frac{T_A}{T_B} \times \text{revs of A} \right)$$

Therefore, the overall V.R. is given by

$$\text{V.R.} = \frac{\text{revs of F}}{\text{revs of A}} = \frac{T_A}{T_B} \times \frac{T_C}{T_D} \times \frac{T_E}{T_F} \tag{6.20}$$

and it can be seen that every wheel contributes to the overall ratio.

Systems of gears are often incorporated with other elements to form a simple machine. An example of this is the *simple winch*, shown in Fig. 6.11.

This employs a gear train to develop the required V.R., with a handle or pulley wheel at the input end and a load drum at the output end. The load is attached to the free end of a cord which is attached to, and coiled around, the load drum. A larger V.R. may be obtained by using a compound gear train instead of the simple train shown, in which case it is called a *compound winch*. An analysis of the operation of the simple winch is given in worked example no. 4.

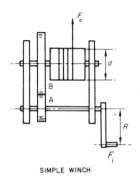

SIMPLE WINCH

Figure 6.11

A different type of geared system is used in the *worm and wheel,* shown in Fig. 6.12.

The worm is similar in appearance to a screw but the thread engages with gear teeth on the wheel. For the system to function, the circular pitch of the teeth on the wheel must be the same as the pitch of the thread on the worm,

$$\text{lead of the worm} = np \quad \text{(see Eq. 6.22)}$$

where p = the common pitch of teeth and thread and n = the number of starts of the worm.

One revolution of the worm will cause each tooth on the wheel to be displaced along the circumference of the wheel a distance equal to the lead of the worm. The corresponding rotation of the wheel will depend on the relationship between this distance and the

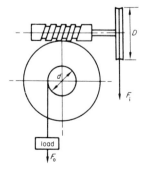

WORM AND WHEEL

Figure 6.12

circumference of the wheel,

$$\text{corresponding revolutions of wheel} = \frac{np}{\text{circumference}} = \frac{np}{Tp} = \frac{n}{T}$$

where T is the total number of teeth on the wheel.

Thus, for one complete revolution of the worm,

$$\text{input displacement of effort} = x_i = \pi D$$

$$\text{output displacement of load} = x_o = \pi d(n/T)$$

$$\text{velocity ratio} = \frac{x_i}{x_o} = \frac{\pi D}{\pi d(n/T)} = \frac{DT}{dn} \qquad (6.21)$$

6.8 The screw-jack

The early Egyptians discovered that very large masses could be raised by pushing them up inclined planes having a shallow gradient. The modern equivalent is the screw thread, in which the inclined plane is 'wrapped' round a cylindrical core, and the same effect achieved by rotation of the *screw* thus formed.

The screw-jack is shown in Fig. 6.13 and consists of a vertical screw, which runs in a fixed 'nut' at the base and carries a circular table at the top. The load is placed on this table and is caused to rise (or fall) when the table is rotated.

If p is the *pitch* of the screw – that is, the distance between corresponding points of adjacent threads – then this is the axial displacement of the screw, and therefore of the load, when the screw makes one complete revolution. This, however, is only true if the screw has a *single-start* thread. A *two-start* thread consists

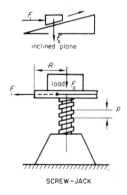

SCREW-JACK

Figure 6.13

essentially of two separate threads arranged alternatively on the cylindrical core of the screw, so that one complete revolution causes it to move an axial distance equal to two pitch lengths. The axial displacement of the screw of one complete revolution is called the *lead* of the screw, and, in general:

$$\text{lead of a screw} = np \tag{6.22}$$

where $p = $ pitch of the screw thread and $n = $ the number of starts.

Let the screw make one complete revolution.

$$\text{Input displacement of effort} = x_i = 2\pi R$$

where R is the radius of the table, or torque arm.

$$\text{Output displacement of load} = x_o = \text{lead of screw} = np$$

$$\text{Velocity ratio} = \frac{x_i}{x_o} = \frac{2\pi R}{np} \tag{6.23}$$

It is frequently not possible for the load to rotate with the screw, and under such circumstances the top of the screw must be allowed to rotate in a fixed collar. This introduces additional friction and must inevitably reduce the efficiency of the machine.

Worked examples

1. A pulley-block arrangement with three pulleys in both upper and lower blocks is used to lift a mass of 150 kg against the pull of gravity. If the effort required is 0.5 kN, calculate the efficiency of the device at this particular load. Assume $g = 9.81 \text{ m/s}^2$.

Since a total of six pulleys is used, the V.R. = 6.

$$\text{load } F_o = mg = 150 \times 9.81 = 1472 \text{ N} = 1.47 \text{ kN}$$
$$\text{effort } F_i = 0.5 \text{ kN}$$

$$\text{M.A.} = \frac{F_o}{F_i} = \frac{1.47}{0.5} = 2.94$$

$$\text{efficiency} = \frac{\text{M.A.}}{\text{V.R.}} = \frac{2.94}{6} = 0.49 = 49\%$$

2. A uniform bar is used as a 2nd-order lever to overcome the weight of a 50 kg mass attached to the bar at a point 300 mm from the fulcrum. The effort is applied at a point 1.2 m from the fulcrum. Assuming no friction, what is the mechanical advantage of this lever if: (a) the mass of the bar is neglected; (b) the mass of the bar is 7 kg?

What is the efficiency in each case?

The lever is similar to that of Fig. 6.5(b).

$$\text{V.R.} = \frac{x_i}{x_o} = \frac{AB}{BC} = \frac{1.2}{0.3} = 4$$

(a) If the mass of the bar is neglected, moments about the fulcrum give

$$F_i \times 1.2 = F_o \times 0.3$$

$$\text{M.A.} = \frac{F_o}{F_i} = \frac{1.2}{0.3} = 4$$

$$\text{efficiency} = \frac{\text{M.A.}}{\text{V.R.}} = \frac{4}{4} = 1.0 = 100\%$$

(b) If the mass of the bar is 7 kg, the effort has to overcome its weight in addition to the load.

$$F_o = \text{weight of the load} = 50\,g = 50 \times 9.81 = 490.5\,\text{N}$$

$$W = \text{weight of the bar} = 7\,g = 7 \times 9.81 = 68.67\,\text{N}$$

Since it is a uniform bar, its weight will act at its mid-point.

Taking moments about the fulcrum,

$$F_i \times 1.2 = (F_o \times 0.3) + (W \times 0.6)$$
$$= (490.5 \times 0.3) + (68.67 \times 0.6)$$
$$= 188.35\,\text{Nm}$$

$$F_i = \frac{188.35}{1.2} = 157\,\text{N}$$

$$\text{M.A.} = \frac{F_o}{F_i} = \frac{490.5}{157} = 3.12$$

$$\text{efficiency} = \frac{\text{M.A.}}{\text{V.R.}} = \frac{3.12}{4} = 0.78 = 78\%$$

3. A compound gear train, similar to that of Fig. 6.10, has the following numbers of teeth on its wheels:

A, 60; B, 15; C, 60; D, 20; E, 48; F, 16.

The effort torque is applied to wheel F, the input power to this wheel being 80 W at a speed of 1000 rev/min. Assuming a 90% transmission efficiency, find the speed and torque available at the output gear wheel A.

What is the mechanical advantage of the gear train?

$$\text{V.R.} = \frac{\text{revs/min of F}}{\text{revs/min of A}} = \frac{60}{15} \times \frac{60}{20} \times \frac{48}{16} = 36$$

$$\frac{1000}{\text{revs/min of A}} = 36$$

$$\text{speed of A} = \frac{1000}{36} = 27.78 \text{ rev/min}$$

power available at the output $A = 0.90 \times 80 \text{ W} = 72 \text{ W}$

torque at $A \times$ speed of $A = 72 \text{ W}$

torque at $A \times (27.78 \times 2\pi/60) = 72 \text{ W}$

torque at $A \times (2.91) = 72 \text{ W}$

$$\text{torque at } A = \frac{72}{2.91} = 24.74 \text{ Nm}$$

Since efficiency = M.A./V.R.,

$$\text{M.A.} = \text{V.R.} \times \text{efficiency}$$

$$= 36 \times 0.90$$

$$= 32.4$$

4. A simple winch, similar to that of Fig. 6.11, has the following particulars: length of effort handle, $R = 250 \text{ mm}$; diameter of load drum, $d = 100 \text{ mm}$; number of teeth on wheel $A = 50$; number of teeth on wheel $B = 250$. What is the ideal effort required to operate the winch against a load of 2 kN? What is the actual effort required to overcome this load, and the corresponding friction effort, if the efficiency is 20%?

With reference to Fig. 6.11, let the effort handle be turned through one complete revolution. Since the wheel A has 50 teeth, the same number of teeth will be engaged on wheel B.

$$\text{Revolutions of wheel B and load drum} = \frac{T_A}{T_B} = \frac{50}{250} = \frac{1}{5}$$

where T_A and T_B are the numbers of teeth on A and B, respectively.

$$\text{Input displacement of effort} = x_i = 2\pi R = 500\pi \text{ mm}$$

$$\text{Output displacement of load} = x_o = \tfrac{1}{5}(\pi d) = 20\pi \text{ mm}$$

$$\text{V.R.} = \frac{x_i}{x_o} = \frac{500\pi}{20\pi} = 25$$

For an ideal machine,

$$\text{efficiency} = \text{M.A.}/\text{V.R.} = 1.0$$

$$\text{ideal M.A.} = \text{V.R.} = 25$$

$$\frac{\text{load}}{\text{ideal effort}} = 25$$

$$\text{ideal effort} = \frac{\text{load}}{25} = \frac{2000}{25} = 80 \text{ N}$$

From Eq. 6.5,

$$\text{actual M.A.} = \eta(\text{V.R.}) = 0.20(25) = 5$$

$$\text{actual effort} = \frac{\text{load}}{5} = \frac{2000}{5} = 400 \text{ N}$$

$$\text{friction effort} = \text{actual effort} - \text{ideal effort}$$

$$= 400 - 80$$

$$= 320 \text{ N}$$

5. A double-start lead screw of 6 mm pitch operates the saddle of a lathe, moving it horizontally along the lathe bed at a constant speed of 15 mm/s. The coefficient of sliding friction is 0.1, the mass of the saddle is 160 kg, and g is 9.81 m/s². Determine the speed of rotation of the lead screw, and, assuming an efficiency of 40%, the torque and power which must be supplied to the screw.

Lead of the screw $= np = 2 \times 6 \text{ mm} = 12 \text{ mm}$. This is the axial displacement for one revolution of the screw.

$$\text{Speed of rotation of the screw} = \frac{\text{speed of advance}}{\text{lead of screw}}$$

$$= \frac{15 \text{ mm/s}}{12 \text{ mm}} = 1.25 \text{ rev/s} = 75 \text{ rev/min}$$

$$\text{gravitational force on saddle} = mg = 160(9.81) = 1570 \text{ N}$$

$$\text{frictional resistance of saddle} = \mu F_N = \mu(mg) = 0.1(1570) = 157 \text{ N}$$

$$\text{power output} = \text{load} \times \text{speed} = 157 \times 0.015 = 2.355 \text{ W}$$

$$\text{efficiency} = \frac{\text{power output}}{\text{power input}}$$

$$\text{power input} = \frac{\text{power output}}{\text{efficiency}} = \frac{2.355}{0.40} = 5.89 \text{ W}$$

But power input $= T\omega$, where T is the torque applied to the lead screw and ω is its angular velocity in rad/s.

$$T(75 \times 2\pi/60) = 5.89 \text{ W}$$

$$T = 5.89/7.854 = 0.75 \text{ N m}$$

6. A screw-jack has a single-start thread with a pitch of 5.5 mm. The jack is operated by means of a torque arm of length 0.7 m. Calculate its velocity ratio.

A load of mass 0.5 tonne was found to require an effort of 50 N applied to the end of the torque arm, while a load of mass 1.5 tonne required an effort of 100 N similarly applied. Assuming a linear relationship between effort and load, and that $g = 10$ m/s², determine the law of the machine.

Hence find: (a) the effort required to lift a load of mass 4 tonne and the efficiency at this load; (b) the limiting values of the mechanical advantage and of the efficiency.

From Eq. 6.23,

$$\text{V.R.} = \frac{2\pi(0.7)}{(5.5 \times 10^{-3})} = 800$$

The law of the machine will be of the form:

$$F_i = aF_o + b$$

where F_i is the effort and F_o ($= mg$) is the gravitional force on the load mass.

Since 1 tonne $= 1000$ kg and $g = 10$ m/s²,

gravitational force on 0.5 tonne mass $= 500 \times 10 = 5000$ N

gravitational force on 1.5 tonne mass $= 1500 \times 10 = 15\,000$ N

Substituting corresponding values of F_i and F_o,

$$50 = a\ 5000 + b$$
$$100 = a\ 15\,000 + b$$

By substraction,

$$50 = 10\,000a$$
$$a = 5 \times 10^{-3} = 0.005$$

Re-substituting,

$$b = 50 - 5000(5 \times 10^{-3}) = 25$$

The law of the machine is:

$$F_i = 0.005\ F_o + 25$$

where F_i and F_o are measured in newtons.

(a) Gravitational force on 4 tonne mass,

$$F_o = 4000 \times 10 = 40\,000 \text{ N}$$

$$\text{effort required} = F_i = 0.005(40\,000) + 25 = 225 \text{ N}$$

$$\text{M.A.} = \frac{F_o}{F_i} = \frac{40\,000}{225} = 178$$

$$\text{efficiency} = \frac{\text{M.A.}}{\text{V.R.}} = \frac{178}{800} = 0.2225 = 22.25\%$$

(b) From Eq. 6.8,

$$\text{M.A.}_{\text{(limiting)}} = \frac{1}{a} = \frac{1}{0.005} = 200$$

From Eq. 6.10,

$$\eta_{\text{(limiting)}} = \frac{(1/a)}{\text{V.R.}} = \frac{200}{800} = 0.25 = 25\%$$

Problems

1. The effective wheel and axle diameters of a wheel and axle are, respectively, 240 mm and 50 mm. Using this machine, a load of mass 60 kg was raised by an effort of 180 N and a 200 kg mass required an effort of 500 N.
Determine the law of this machine, and also the maximum efficiency theoretically possible. Take $g = 9.81$ m/s^2.

(*Answer.* $F_i = (0.233F_o + 43)$N, 89.4%.)

2. (a) A bar 1.5 m long is used as a 1st-order lever to raise a mass of 100 kg. Load and effort are at the extreme ends of the bar. How far from the load end of the bar must the fulcrum be positioned if the effort is to be limited to 40 N?
(b) A 3rd-order lever, pivoted at one end, carries a load of 50 N at the other end. If the lever is 400 m long, what effort is required at a point 120 mm from the pivot?

(*Answer.* (a) 59 mm; (b) 167 N.)

3. A set of pulley blocks has four pulleys in the upper block and three in the lower. Using this lifting tackle, an effort of 120 N is required to raise a mass of 60 kg against the force of gravity. Calculate the efficiency of the device at this load, and also the effort required to overcome friction. Assume $g = 9.81$ m/s^2.

(*Answer.* 70.1%, 35.9 N.)

4. (a) Three gear wheels, A, B, and C, have 20 teeth, 50 teeth, and 90 teeth, respectively. They are arranged as a simple gear train with A as the input while C carries the load torque. Assuming 100% efficiency, what will be the mechanical advantage of the system?
(b) A compound train is made up of four wheels, A, B, C, and D. A is the input wheel and has 24 teeth. B and C have 60 and 20 teeth, respectively, and are keyed to the same shaft. D has 50 teeth. Wheel A meshes with B, while C drives the load wheel D. Assuming a transmission efficiency of 80%, calculate the velocity ratio and mechanical advantage of the gear train.

(*Answer.* (a) 4.5; (b) 6.25, 5.0.)

5. A screw-jack has a single-start thread of 11 mm pitch. The axis of the screw is vertical, and the load is carried on a circular table of diameter 490 mm. The jack is operated by rotating the table, by means of a cord wrapped around its rim, as shown in Fig. 6.13. With a mass of 175 kg on the table, an effort of 50 N is required to make it rise.

Assuming $g = 10$ m/s^2, calculate the efficiency at this load and the work done against friction when the table rises 100 mm.

(*Answer.* 25%, 525 J.)

6. In a test on a machine to determine its characteristics, the following results were obtained:

Load (kN)	1.0	3.0	5.0	7.0	9.0
Effort (kN)	0.165	0.290	0.425	0.555	0.685

The velocity ratio of the machine is 32.

From these results, deduce the law of the machine. Hence deduce the limiting values of the mechanical advantage and the efficiency, and state whether under any conditions it is possible for the machine to overhaul.

Draw graphs showing the variation of efficiency and friction effort with load. What is the friction effort when the load is 8 kN?

(*Answer.* $F_i = (0.065F_o + 100)$ N, 15.38, 48%, 0.37 kN.)

7. A worm-and-wheel lifting device has a two-start worm and a wheel with 60 teeth. The load drum keyed to the wheel shaft has a diameter of 0.25 m. Assuming an efficiency of 40%, determine the torque required at the worm shaft to raise a load of mass 200 kg against the pull of gravity. Assume $g = 9.81$ m/s^2.

(*Answer.* 20.4 N m.)

8. A winch is used to drag a mass of 2 tonnes up a plane inclined at 20° to the horizontal. The winch is arranged at the top of the incline so that the cable is parallel to the plane. The coefficient of friction between the mass and the plane is 0.3 and g may be taken to be $10 \, \text{m/s}^2$.

The input member of the winch is driven by an electric motor at a constant speed of 500 rev/min, and compound gearing between the motor and the 200 mm diameter load drum gives a reduction of 50 to 1. Assuming the efficiency of the machine is 15%, find: (a) the speed of the 2 tonne mass up the incline; (b) the torque applied by the motor to the input member of the winch; (c) the power supplied by the motor.

(*Answer.* (a) 0.1047 m/s (b) 166.4 N m (c) 8.71 kW.)

7. Electrical circuits

7.1 Charge, current, potential difference, and electromotive force

The basic component of all matter is the atom, and this consists of a nucleus surrounded by electrons. One important property of these elementary particles is that they are electrically charged – the nucleus has a positive charge and each electron has a negative charge. Normally the positive charge on the nucleus equals the negative charge on the electrons so that the atom as a whole is electrically neutral, but if some of the atoms in an object contain extra electrons the object will possess a negative charge (alternatively, if electrons have been removed from some of the atoms in an object it will have a positive charge).

If a negatively charged object (i.e., one having a surplus of electrons) is connected to a positively charged object by an electrical conductor, the surplus electrons will commence to move from atom to atom along the conductor in order to reach the positively charged object and make good its deficiency in electrons, and this movement of electrons constitutes an electric current. Thus an electric current consists of a movement of charge and the magnitude of the current is the rate of movement of charge, or (for a steady current),

$$\text{current } I = \frac{Q}{t} \tag{7.1}$$

where Q = charge flowing past a given point in time t.

Logically, the basic unit of charge would be the charge possessed by an individual electron; but this would be far too small for practical purposes – the smallest electric currents (in electronic circuits, for example) involve very large numbers of individual electrons. Hence the practical unit of charge, the coulomb (C) is based on the SI unit of current, the ampere (A). The coulomb is defined as the quantity of charge which flows past a point in a circuit in one second when the current in the circuit is one ampere. (This corresponds, in fact, to about 6×10^{18} electrons.) Thus,

$$1 \text{ ampere} = 1 \text{ coulomb/second}$$

and

$$1 \text{ coulomb} = 1 \text{ ampere second}$$

In order to cause a current to flow, a 'driving force' or 'electrical pressure' is required and this is measured in volts (V). It is commonly referred to simply as 'voltage' but may be described in two slightly different ways – as a 'potential difference' (symbol V) or as an 'electromotive force' (usually abbreviated to e.m.f. and given the symbol E). The term 'potential difference' is applied to the voltage between any two points in a circuit, and would be measured by connecting a voltmeter between these points. Every circuit, however, must contain an energy source such as a battery and the term 'electromotive force' refers to the 'driving force' provided by this source. Usually this *cannot* be measured by a voltmeter since if a current is flowing, some of the e.m.f. will be required to make the current flow through the source itself and only the remainder will appear at the source terminals (see Section 7.4).

Voltage has been described as 'electrical pressure' but as a *definition* this is unsatisfactory and the volt is in fact defined in terms of energy. In order to make a current flow round a circuit, energy must be expended (and, if the circuit is made up simply of resistors, this energy will be converted into heat). Thus the definition of the volt is that 1 joule of energy is required when 1 coulomb of charge flows across a potential difference of 1 volt.

From this, it follows that the potential difference between two points may be defined as the energy required to move one coulomb of charge through the circuit between these points. Similarly, the e.m.f. of a source is the total electrical energy produced by it per coulomb of charge flowing round the circuit.

7.2 Ohm's law

This law was originally stated in the form: 'The current I in a conductor is directly proportional to the potential difference V between its ends, provided that physical conditions (in particular, temperature) remain constant'.

$$I \propto V$$

or

$$I = \frac{V}{\text{a constant}}$$

This constant is called the *resistance* of the conductor (symbol R) so

139

that the relationship may be expressed as:

$$I = \frac{V}{R} \qquad (7.2)$$

or, transposing,

$$V = IR \qquad (7.3)$$

or

$$R = \frac{V}{I} \qquad (7.4)$$

These expressions are, in fact often referred to as 'Ohm's law' but it should be pointed out that this is not strictly true. They follow logically from the law but Ohm's law is concerned with the direct proportionality of current and voltage, and is not obeyed by all resistors. There are many conductors – semiconductors in particular – for which current is not proportional to applied voltage. (These are termed 'non-linear' since for them the graph of current against voltage is not a straight line.) It is, however, possible to use expressions such as $V = IR$ in all cases by regarding R as 'the resistance offered by the circuit to the flow of current', and by realizing that in the case of a non-linear resistor, R will not have a constant value. An electric lamp, for example, is a non-linear resistor and the lack of proportionality between current and voltage may be explained by saying that as the temperature of the lamp filament rises, its resistance increases.

The unit of resistance is the ohm (Ω) and its definition follows from the relationship $R = V/I$; thus

$$1 \text{ ohm} = 1 \text{ volt per ampere}$$

7.3 Resistors in series and parallel

Electrical components may be connected together in two ways; 'in series' (Fig. 7.1) or 'in parallel' (Fig. 7.2.). It will be seen that for two resistors in series, the same current flows through both resistors, but the potential difference across each is only part of the total voltage; while for two resistors in parallel, each has the same applied voltage but takes only part of the total current. For purposes

Figure 7.1

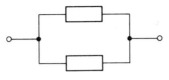

Figure 7.2

of calculation it is convenient to find, in each case, the 'equivalent resistance'; that is, the value of a single resistor which could replace the series or parallel combination.

For any number of resistors in series, the equivalent resistance is simply the sum of the individual resistances. This may be shown by referring to Fig. 7.3. Applying Eq. 7.3 to each resistor in turn,

$$V_1 = IR_1, \ V_2 = IR_2, \text{ and } V_3 = IR_3$$

Applied voltage $V = V_1 + V_2 + V_3$
$$= IR_1 + IR_2 + IR_3$$
$$= I(R_1 + R_2 + R_3)$$

Hence from Eq. 7.4,

$$\text{equivalent resistance } R = \frac{V}{I} = \frac{I(R_1 + R_2 + R_3)}{I}$$

or

$$R = R_1 + R_2 + R_3 \tag{7.5}$$

For resistors in parallel, the equivalent resistance will be *smaller* than any of the individual resistances since placing resistors in parallel offers the current alternative paths and makes it *easier* for current to flow through the circuit as a whole. Referring to Fig. 7.4,

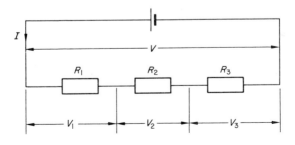

Figure 7.3

7. ELECTRICAL CIRCUITS

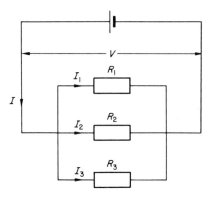

Figure 7.4

and applying Eq. 7.2 to each resistor in turn,

$$I_1 = \frac{V}{R_1}, \ I_2 = \frac{V}{R_2}, \text{ and } I_3 = \frac{V}{R_3}$$

Total current $I = I_1 + I_2 + I_3$

$$= \frac{V}{R_1} + \frac{V}{R_2} + \frac{V}{R_3}$$

$$= V\left(\frac{1}{R_1} + \frac{1}{R_2} + \frac{1}{R_3}\right)$$

For a single resistance R, current would be given by $I = V/R$
Hence

$$\frac{V}{R} = V\left(\frac{1}{R_1} + \frac{1}{R_2} + \frac{1}{R_3}\right)$$

or

$$\frac{1}{R} = \frac{1}{R_1} + \frac{1}{R_2} + \frac{1}{R_3} \tag{7.6}$$

Worked examples

1. If 100 C flow past a point in a circuit in 20 s, what is the current?

$$I = \frac{Q}{t}$$

$$= \frac{100}{20} = 5 \text{ A}$$

2. The current flowing in a circuit is 50 mA. What quantity of charge will have flowed past a point in the circuit in 1 minute?

$$I = \frac{Q}{t}$$

hence

$$Q = It$$
$$= 50 \times 10^{-3} \times 60$$
$$= 3 \text{ C}$$

3. What is the potential difference across a circuit if 40 J of energy is expended in causing 2 C of charge to flow round it?

potential difference = energy per coulomb

$$= \frac{40}{2} = 20 \text{ V}$$

4. What current will flow through a 25 Ω resistor when there is a potential difference of 100 V across its ends?

$$I = \frac{V}{R}$$
$$= \frac{100}{25} = 4 \text{ A}$$

5. A current of 20 mA flows through a 3 kΩ resistor. What will be the potential difference across the resistor?

$$V = IR$$
$$= 20 \times 10^{-3} \times 3 \times 10^{3}$$
$$= 60 \text{ V}$$

6. In order to find the resistance of a component, the circuit shown in Fig. 7.5 is used. If the ammeter reads 1.6 A and the voltmeter reads 12 V, what is the resistance R?

$$R = \frac{V}{I}$$
$$= \frac{12}{1.6} = 7.5 \text{ Ω}$$

7. Three resistors of value 20 Ω, 30 Ω, and 40 Ω respectively are connected (a) in series, (b) in parallel. Find, in each case, the equivalent resistance and the current which will flow if a battery

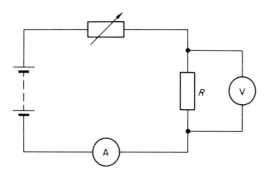

Figure 7.5

having a terminal voltage of 45 V is connected to the combination.

The circuits are shown in Figs. 7.6(a) and 7.6(b).

(a)
$$R = R_1 + R_2 + R_3$$
$$= 20 + 30 + 40$$
$$= 90 \ \Omega$$
$$I = \frac{V}{R}$$
$$= \frac{45}{90} = 0.5 \ A$$

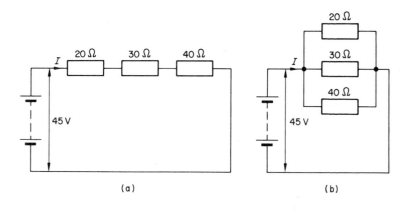

Figure 7.6

(b)
$$\frac{1}{R} = \frac{1}{R_1} + \frac{1}{R_2} + \frac{1}{R_3}$$

$$= \frac{1}{20} + \frac{1}{30} + \frac{1}{40}$$

$$= \frac{6+4+3}{120} = \frac{13}{120}$$

$$R = \frac{120}{13} = 9.23 \, \Omega$$

$$I = \frac{V}{R}$$

$$= \frac{45}{9.23} = 4.875 \text{ A}$$

8. For the circuit shown in Fig. 7.7, calculate: (a) the current taken from the battery; (b) the potential difference across each resistor.

$$\text{Equivalent resistance } R = R_1 + R_2$$

$$= 50 + 100$$

$$= 150 \, \Omega$$

(a)
$$\text{Current from battery, } I = \frac{V}{R}$$

$$= \frac{30}{150}$$

$$= 0.2 \text{ A or } 200 \text{ mA}$$

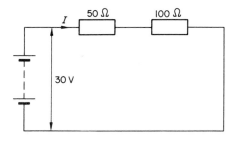

Figure 7.7

(b)   For the 50 Ω resistor, $V = IR$
$$= 0.2 \times 50$$
$$= 10\,\text{V}$$

For the 100 Ω resistor, $V = IR$
$$= 0.2 \times 100$$
$$= 20\,\text{V}$$

It will be seen that the total potential difference is divided in the ratio of the resistances, or, potential difference across any resistor is proportional to its resistance; this applies to any number of resistors in series.

9. For the circuit shown in Fig. 7.8, find: (a) the current taken from the battery; (b) the current in each resistor.

(a) $$\frac{1}{R} = \frac{1}{R_1} + \frac{1}{R_2}$$
$$= \frac{1}{30} + \frac{1}{60} = \frac{3}{60}$$

Hence equivalent resistance $R = \dfrac{60}{3} = 20\,\Omega$

Current from battery, $I = \dfrac{V}{R}$
$$= \frac{30}{20} = 1.5\,\text{A}$$

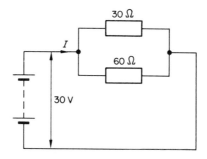

Figure 7.8

(b) Each resistor has a potential difference of 30 V across it, hence:

$$\text{current in } 30 \, \Omega \text{ resistor, } I = \frac{V}{R}$$

$$= \frac{30}{30} = 1 \text{ A}$$

$$\text{current in } 60 \, \Omega \text{ resistor, } I = \frac{V}{R}$$

$$= \frac{30}{60} = 0.5 \text{ A}$$

It will be seen that the current divides so that the current in each resistor is proportional to the resistance of the other. This will be true for any parallel combination of two (but not more than two) resistors.

10. For the circuit shown in Fig. 7.9, find: (a) the current taken from the battery; (b) the potential difference across the 5 Ω resistor; (c) the current in the 12 Ω resistor.

(a) Equivalent resistance of the parallel combination:

$$\frac{1}{R} = \frac{1}{R_1} + \frac{1}{R_2}$$

$$= \frac{1}{12} + \frac{1}{6} = \frac{3}{12}$$

$$R = \frac{12}{3} = 4 \, \Omega$$

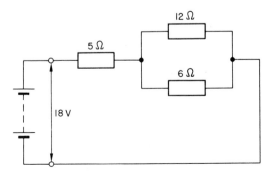

Figure 7.9

147

We may now consider the circuit to consist of a 5 Ω resistor in series with a 4 Ω resistor, so that:
equivalent resistance of whole circuit,

$$R = R_1 + R_2$$
$$= 5 + 4 = 9 \, \Omega$$

Current taken from battery,

$$I = \frac{V}{R}$$
$$= \frac{18}{9} = 2 \, \text{A}$$

(b)   For the 5 Ω resistor, $I = 2$ A
$$V = IR$$
$$= 2 \times 5 = 10 \, \text{V}$$

(c) If the potential difference across the 5 Ω resistor is 10 V and the potential difference across the whole circuit is 18 V, the voltage across the parallel combination must be $(18 - 10) = 8$ V.
For the 12 Ω resistor,

$$I = \frac{V}{R}$$
$$= \frac{8}{12} = 0.667 \, \text{A}$$

11. For the circuit shown in Fig. 7.10, find the current flowing in each resistor.

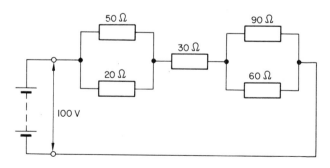

Figure 7.10

For the 50 Ω and 20 Ω parallel combination:

$$\frac{1}{R} = \frac{1}{R_1} + \frac{1}{R_2}$$

$$= \frac{1}{50} + \frac{1}{20} = \frac{2+5}{100} = \frac{7}{100}$$

$$R = \frac{100}{7} = 14.29 \, \Omega$$

For the 90 Ω and 60 Ω parallel combination:

$$\frac{1}{R} = \frac{1}{R_1} + \frac{1}{R_2}$$

$$= \frac{1}{90} + \frac{1}{60} = \frac{2+3}{180} = \frac{5}{180}$$

$$R = \frac{180}{5} = 36 \, \Omega$$

Treating the circuit as three resistors in series,

$$R = R_1 + R_2 + R_3$$

$$= 14.29 + 30 + 36$$

$$= 80.29 \, \Omega$$

Hence current taken from supply,

$$I = \frac{V}{R}$$

$$= \frac{100}{80.29} = 1.246 \, A$$

This will be the current in the 30 Ω resistor. The 50 Ω–20 Ω parallel combination could be replaced by a single resistor of value 14.29 Ω (i.e., the equivalent resistance). Hence the voltage across this combination will be given by $V = IR$ where $R =$ equivalent resistance.

$$V = 1.246 \times 14.29$$

$$= 17.8 \, V$$

Hence for the 50 Ω resistor,

$$I = \frac{V}{R}$$

$$= \frac{17.8}{50} = 0.356 \, A$$

and for the 20 Ω resistor,

$$I = \frac{V}{R}$$

$$= \frac{17.8}{20} = 0.89 \text{ A}$$

Voltage across the 90 Ω–60 Ω parallel combination (equivalent resistance 36 Ω):

$$V = IR$$

$$= 1.246 \times 36$$

$$= 44.86 \text{ V}$$

Hence for the 90 Ω resistor,

$$I = \frac{V}{R}$$

$$= \frac{44.86}{90} = 0.498 \text{ A}$$

and for the 60 Ω resistor,

$$I = \frac{V}{R}$$

$$= \frac{44.86}{60} = 0.748 \text{ A}$$

7.4. Internal resistance and terminal potential difference

If a current is to flow in an electrical circuit, it must include a source of e.m.f. For simple circuits there will only be one such source, and the e.m.f. will usually be generated chemically in a battery, or by electromagnetic induction in a mechanically driven generator. (There are, in fact, other ways of generating an e.m.f. – solar cells, for example.) All sources, however, will possess *internal resistance*. In a battery-powered circuit, for example, the current flowing round the external circuit must also flow through the battery itself, and in doing so will meet with resistance as it passes through the various components which make up the battery. This resistance is in fact inseparable from the source of e.m.f., but for purposes of calculation the battery (or other source) may be thought of as consisting of a source of e.m.f. E in series with a resistance R_{INT} as in Fig. 7.11.

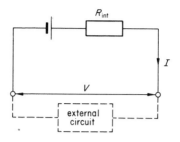

Figure 7.11

When a current I flows, there will be a 'voltage drop' across the internal resistance which, from Eq. 7.3, will be equal to IR_{INT}. Hence the terminal potential difference V_T will be given by

$$V_T = E - IR_{INT} \tag{7.7}$$

It will be seen that if $I = 0$, $V_T = E$. In other words, if no current is being taken from a source, its terminal voltage will be equal to its e.m.f., or the e.m.f. of a source is equal to its open-circuit terminal voltage. Thus the e.m.f. of, say, a battery may, for practical purposes, be found by disconnecting it from any external circuit and connecting a high-resistance voltmeter across its terminals.

Worked examples

12. A battery has an e.m.f. of 6 V and an internal resistance of 1.5 Ω. What will be its terminal potential difference when supplying a current of 200 mA?

$$V_T = E - IR_{INT}$$
$$= 6 - (200 \times 10^{-3} \times 1.5)$$
$$= 6 - 0.3$$
$$= 5.7 \text{ V}$$

13. The battery in example 12 is connected to two resistors of values 12 Ω and 20 Ω arranged in parallel. What will be the current taken from the battery and what will be its terminal voltage?

Representing the battery as a source of e.m.f. in series with an internal resistance, the circuit will be as shown in Fig. 7.12.

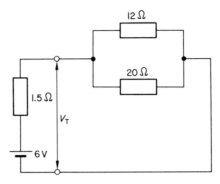

Figure 7.12

For the parallel combination,

$$\frac{1}{R} = \frac{1}{R_1} + \frac{1}{R_2}$$

$$= \frac{1}{12} + \frac{1}{20} = \frac{5+3}{60} = \frac{8}{60}$$

$$R = \frac{60}{8} = 7.5 \ \Omega$$

Hence total circuit resistance

$$R = R_1 + R_2$$
$$= 1.5 + 7.5$$
$$= 9 \ \Omega$$

Current from battery,

$$I = \frac{V}{R}$$

$$= \frac{6}{9} = 0.667 \ \text{A}$$

Terminal voltage,

$$V_T = E - IR_{INT}$$
$$= 6 - (0.667 \times 1.5)$$
$$= 6 - 1$$
$$= 5 \ \text{V}$$

14. A generator has an open-circuit voltage of 240 V. When it is connected to a circuit taking 20 A, its terminal voltage falls to 230 V. What is its internal resistance?

$$V_T = E - IR_{INT}$$

The open-circuit voltage of a source is equal to its e.m.f., hence in this case $E = 240$ V, and

$$230 = 240 - 20R_{INT}$$
$$20R_{INT} = 10$$
$$R_{INT} = 0.5 \ \Omega$$

Problems

1. In a circuit, 150 C flow past a point in 100 s. What is the current?

(*Answer.* 1.5 A.)

2. If a charge of 3 C flows through a resistor during a period of 10 minutes, what current is flowing?

(*Answer.* 5 mA.)

3. If the current in a conductor is 0.6 A, what quantity of charge will flow past a given point in 20 s?

(*Answer.* 12 C.)

4. What charge will flow through a circuit if a current of 100 μA flows for 1 minute?

(*Answer.* 6 mC.)

5. A current of 2 mA flows into a capacitor for a period of 2 minutes. What charge will the capacitor have received?

(*Answer.* 0.24 C.)

6. A conductor carries a current of 25 mA. In what period of time will 10 C flow past a given point?

(*Answer.* 6 min 40 s.)

7. What is the potential difference across a resistor if 100 J of energy are expended in causing 2.5 C of charge to flow through it?

(*Answer.* 40 V.)

8. A battery has an e.m.f. of 12 V. How much electrical energy will it have produced when 50 C have flowed through it?

(*Answer.* 600 J.)

9. An electric fire element has a resistance of 60 Ω. What current will flow when it is connected to a 240 V supply?

(*Answer.* 4 A.)

10. A battery having a terminal voltage of 9 V is connected to a 1.8 kΩ resistor. What will be the current and what charge will flow through the resistor in 1 minute?

(*Answer.* 5 mA, 0.3 C.)

11. A current of 0.5 A flows through a resistor and the potential difference across it is 75 V. What is its resistance?

(*Answer.* 150 Ω.)

12. A motor vehicle headlamp takes a current of 3 A when connected to a 12 V supply. What is its resistance?

(*Answer.* 4 Ω.)

13. The voltage between the two conductors of a cable is 500 V and the current 'leaking' through the insulation between them is 20 μA. What is the insulation resistance?

(*Answer.* 25 MΩ.)

14. A current of 3 A flows through a circuit whose total resistance is 20 Ω. What will be the potential difference across the circuit?

(*Answer.* 60 V.)

15. The cable connecting a motor vehicle battery to its starter motor has a resistance of 0.0016 Ω, and the starter takes a current of 200 A. What will be the voltage drop along the cable?

(*Answer.* 0.32 V.)

16. Three resistors of value 4 Ω, 6 Ω, and 12 Ω respectively are connected (a) in series, (b) in parallel. Find, in each case, the equivalent resistance.

(*Answer.* (a) 22 Ω (b) 2 Ω.)

17. Three resistors of value 18 Ω, 50 Ω, and 32 Ω respectively are connected in series across a 150 V supply. Find the current flowing and the voltage across each resistor.

(*Answer.* 1.5 A; 27 V, 75 V and 48 V.)

18. Two lamps are connected in parallel to a 240 V supply. If their resistances are respectively 570 Ω and 960 Ω, what will be the total current taken from the supply?

(*Answer.* 0.671 A.)

19. An electric blanket has two elements, each of resistance 500 Ω. It is fitted with a three-heat switch which operates as follows: 'low' – both elements in series; 'medium' – one element only; 'high' – both elements in parallel. If connected to a 240 V supply, what current would flow for each position?

(*Answer.* 0.24 A, 0.48 A, 0.96 A.)

20. A 30 Ω resistor is connected in parallel with a 50 Ω resistor, and this combination is connected in series with a 20 Ω resistor across a 100 V supply. Find: (a) the current taken from the supply; (b) the current in the 50 Ω resistor.

(*Answer.* (a) 2.58 A (b) 0.968 A.)

21. A group of three resistors, of values 12 Ω, 16 Ω, and 20 Ω, is connected in parallel. A 15 Ω resistor is connected in series with this group and the circuit thus formed is connected to a 60 V supply. Find: (a) the current in the 15 Ω resistor; (b) the potential difference across the 12 Ω resistor; and (c) the current in the 16 Ω resistor.

(*Answer.* (a) 2.984 A (b) 15.24 V (c) 0.952 A.)

22. A 15 Ω resistor and a 25 Ω resistor are connected in parallel. This group, a 5 Ω resistor, and an 8 Ω resistor are then connected in series across a 24 V supply. Find: (a) the current taken from the supply; (b) the voltage across the 8 Ω resistor; and (c) the current in the 15 Ω resistor.

(*Answer.* (a) 1.073 A (b) 8.581 V (c) 0.671 A.)

23. A circuit is shown in Fig. 7.13. Find: (a) the current taken from the supply; (b) the current in the 15 Ω resistor; and (c) the current in the 30 Ω resistor.

(*Answer.* (a) 1.75 A (b) 1 A (c) 0.7 A.)

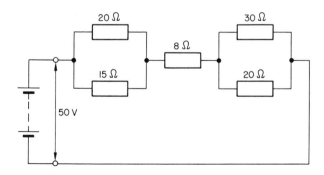

Figure 7.13

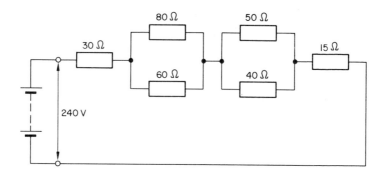

Figure 7.14

24. For the circuit shown in Fig. 7.14 find: (a) the current in the 30 Ω resistor; (b) the voltage across the 15 Ω resistor; (c) the current in the 60 Ω resistor; and (d) the current in the 50 Ω resistor.

(*Answer.* (a) 2.364 A (b) 34.47 V (c) 1.351 A (d) 1.051 A.)

25. For the circuit shown in Fig. 7.15 find: (a) the current taken from the supply; (b) the current in the 8 Ω resistor; and (c) the current in the 7 Ω resistor.

(*Answer.* (a) 3.798 A (b) 1.651 A (c) 2.399 A.)

26. A motor vehicle battery has an e.m.f. of 12.4 V and an internal resistance of 0.015 Ω. What will be the potential difference across its terminals when supplying: (a) a current of 10 A to the lighting circuit; (b) a current of 200 A to the starter?

(*Answer.* (a) 12.25 V (b) 9.4 V.)

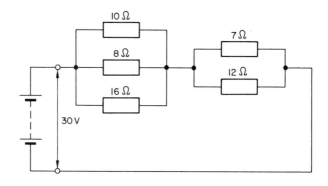

Figure 7.15

27. A voltmeter connected to a generator reads 125 V on no-load, and when the generator is supplying a current of 30 A the voltmeter reads 113 V. What is the internal resistance of the generator?

(*Answer.* 0.4 Ω.)

28. A battery having an e.m.f. of 9 V and an internal resistance of 14 Ω is connected to a 200 Ω resistor. What will be its terminal voltage?

(*Answer.* 8.411 V.)

29. A battery is connected to a high-resistance voltmeter and a reading of 24 V observed. A 14 Ω resistor is connected across its terminals and the voltmeter now reads 21 V. What is the internal resistance of the battery?

(*Answer.* 2 Ω.)

30. A circuit consists of a 10 Ω resistor in series with a parallel combination of a 16 Ω resistor and a 12 Ω resistor. If this circuit is connected to a battery of e.m.f. 20 V and internal resistance 1.5 Ω, what current will be taken from the battery and what will be the potential difference across its terminals?

(*Answer.* 1.089 A, 18.37 V.)

8. Electrical instruments

8.1 The basic meter movement

In order to obtain information about electrical circuits, two basic kinds of measurement are required: of current, and of potential difference. Current is measured by an ammeter, which is connected in series with the circuit so that the current passes through it, and potential difference by a voltmeter connected across the points between which potential difference is to be measured, i.e., in parallel with that portion of the circuit.

The introduction of a measuring instrument will inevitably have some effect on the circuit – an ammeter introduces additional resistance into the circuit while a voltmeter takes a small current – and to minimize these effects (called 'loading errors') it is essential that the resistance of an ammeter is as low as possible, and the resistance of a voltmeter as high as possible.

Meters (apart from digital instruments) contain a 'meter movement' in which the electrical input is converted into movement of a pointer over a scale. Usually this is done by making use of the magnetic effect of an electric current, and there are two kinds of meter movement which work in this way; they are known as 'moving-coil' and 'moving-iron' instruments and their operation will be described in Chapter 9. It should be noted that both types are essentially current-measuring devices; if a voltage is to be measured, it is applied to a circuit of high resistance and the meter is operated by the resulting current which is, by Ohm's law, proportional to the applied voltage.

Although it is possible to use a meter movement which measures current or voltage directly (and this is often done in the case of moving-iron instruments), this cannot normally be done in the case of a moving-coil instrument; it is impractical to design such a meter movement for currents larger than a few milliamps, and the potential difference across the coil cannot be made more than a very small fraction of a volt. The usual procedure is, in fact, to use a meter movement designed for maximum sensitivity; a typical moving-coil instrument will give full-scale deflection (f.s.d) for a current of

$100\,\mu$A and many operate on currents smaller than this. For the measurement of larger currents, the meter movement is connected to a 'shunt' and for voltage measurement a series resistor or 'multiplier' is used.

8.2 Ammeters and shunts

A moving-coil ammeter will normally be used to measure a current much larger than that for which its movement is designed, and this is done by placing a resistor (called a 'shunt') in parallel with the meter movement as in Fig. 8.1. The current will divide so that most of it passes through the shunt and only a small proportion passes through the meter movement. This proportion will depend on the relationship between the resistance of the meter movement and the resistance of the shunt: if, for example, the resistance of the shunt is made equal to the resistance of the meter movement the current will divide equally and half the total current will flow through the meter movement. Thus, a movement having an f.s.d. of $100\,\mu$A will now give f.s.d. for a total current of $200\,\mu$A – in other words, the meter now has a range 0–$200\,\mu$A. By using a shunt of suitable resistance, the meter can have any desired range. For example, a meter scaled 0–10 A may well have a movement giving f.s.d. for 1 mA. In this case, the shunt will be of very low resistance so that when the meter is measuring a current of 10 A, 9.999 A will flow through the shunt and 1 mA through the meter movement.

8.3 Voltmeters and multipliers

A moving-coil voltmeter is in fact a circuit containing a meter movement which measures current: but this current will, by Ohm's law, be directly proportional to the applied voltage. If, for example, a movement giving f.s.d. for a current of $100\,\mu$A and having a resistance of $50\,\Omega$ is used, the voltage across the movement for the

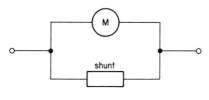

Figure 8.1

Figure 8.2

full-scale current of $100\ \mu$A will be given by

$$V = IR$$
$$= 100 \times 10^{-6} \times 50$$
$$= 5 \times 10^{-3}\ \text{V or }5\ \text{mV}$$

Hence, for direct connection of the meter movement, the instrument could be regarded as a voltmeter having a range 0–5 mV. Normally a much larger range will be required and this is obtained by placing a resistor in series with the meter movement, as in Fig. 8.2. If, say, a range 0–10 V is required, the value of the series resistor R may be found by applying the equation $V = IR$ to the whole circuit (which consists of the resistor R is series with a meter movement of resistance 50 Ω).

$$V = IR$$
$$10 = 100 \times 10^{-6} \times (R + 50)$$
$$R + 50 = \frac{10}{100 \times 10^{-6}}$$
$$= 10^5\ \Omega\ \text{or}\ 100\ \text{k}\Omega$$
$$R = 99.95\ \text{k}\Omega$$

Thus, by using a 99.95 kΩ series resistor, the range of the instrument has been changed from 5 mV to 10 V, i.e., multiplied by a factor of 2000. For this reason, such series resistors are called 'multipliers' and by using a suitable multiplier the instrument can have any desired range.

It may be noted that the smaller the current required by the meter movement, the larger will be the value of the multiplier required for a given range. Since the resistance of a voltmeter should be as high as possible, it follows that the more sensitive the meter movement, the better the voltmeter.

8.4 The ohm-meter

A moving-coil meter can be scaled so as to give a direct measurement of resistance, and it is then called an ohm-meter. A simple ohmmeter circuit is shown in Fig. 8.3. The meter movement is connected in series with a battery, a resistor R_1, and the resistance R which is to be measured. The resistor R_1 is made variable so that small variations in battery voltage can be allowed for.

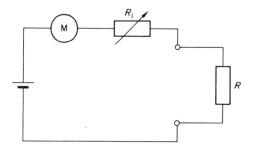

Figure 8.3

Often the battery used is a small single cell giving about 1.5 V, but for convenience let us assume a 1 V supply voltage, a meter movement of 10 Ω resistance giving f.s.d for a current of 1 mA, and a resistor R_1 of value 990 Ω. When the value of the external resistance R is zero (i.e., when the terminals are short-circuited) the meter current will be given by

$$I = \frac{V}{R}$$

$$= \frac{1}{(10+990)}$$

$$= \frac{1}{1000} \text{ A or 1 mA}$$

In other words, the meter will read full-scale and this is marked zero on the resistance scale. (In practice, the battery voltage will vary from time to time and, before making a measurement of resistance, the procedure is to short-circuit the meter terminals and to adjust R_1 until the pointer gives f.s.d., i.e., indicates zero resistance.)

If now a component of resistance 1 kΩ is connected across the ohm-meter terminals, the total resistance in the circuit will be $(10+990+1000) = 2000 \, \Omega$ and the current will be

$$I = \frac{V}{R}$$

$$= \frac{1}{2000} \text{ A or 0.5 mA}$$

Thus, the meter will read half-scale and this point may be marked '1 kΩ'. Proceeding in this way, a complete scale may be constructed. It will read from right to left, having zero corresponding to full-scale meter deflection and infinity corresponding to zero current, and such a scale is shown in Fig. 8.4.

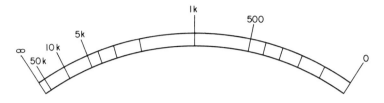

Figure 8.4

8.5 The multimeter

As will have been seen in Sections 8.2, 8.3, and 8.4, the same basic meter movement can be used to indicate current, voltage, or resisance. A 'multimeter' consists of a moving-coil meter movement, together with a selection of shunts and multipliers which (usually by means of switches) may be connected so as to obtain a number of current and voltage ranges. It will also be possible to connect the meter movement into an ohm-meter circuit of the kind described in Section 8.4 and often this circuit may be modified so as to obtain more than one range of resistance measurement.

Most multimeters will also include alternating current and voltage ranges. The meter movement itself is suitable for direct current only–if a current is passed through the moving coil in the opposite direction the pointer will be deflected in the opposite direction, and if an alternating current is passed through the meter movement the pointer will vibrate about the zero position. Thus, when a.c. quantities are to be measured, a rectifier is switched into the circuit so that although the current at the meter terminals is alternating, the current through the meter movement is always in the same direction.

Worked examples

1. A circuit of resistance 1 Ω is connected to a 10 V supply. What will be the current when an ammeter of resistance (a) 0.05 Ω, (b) 0.001 Ω, is connected in series with the circuit?

(a) The total resistance is now

$$R = R_1 + R_2$$
$$= 1 + 0.05$$
$$= 1.05 \ \Omega$$

Hence,

$$\text{current } I = \frac{V}{R}$$

$$= \frac{10}{1.05} = 0.9524 \text{ A}$$

(b)   Total resistance $= 1.001 \ \Omega$

Hence,

$$\text{current } I = \frac{10}{1.001} = 0.9991 \text{ A}$$

2. Two $2 \text{ k}\Omega$ resistors are connected in series across a 40 V supply. What will be the reading of a voltmeter placed across one of them if the voltmeter resistance is (a) $10 \text{ k}\Omega$, (b) $1 \text{ M}\Omega$?

The circuit is shown in Fig. 8.5.
(a) For the parallel combination of voltmeter and $2 \text{ k}\Omega$ resistor,

$$\frac{1}{R} = \frac{1}{R_1} + \frac{1}{R_2}$$

$$= \frac{1}{10 \times 10^3} + \frac{1}{2 \times 10^3}$$

$$= \frac{1+5}{10 \times 10^3} = \frac{6}{10 \times 10^3}$$

$$R = \frac{10 \times 10^3}{6} = 1667 \ \Omega$$

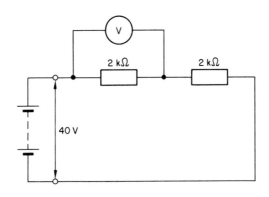

Figure 8.5

Total resistance of circuit,

$$R = R_1 + R_2$$
$$= 1667 + 2000$$
$$= 3667 \ \Omega$$

Current from battery,

$$I = \frac{V}{R}$$
$$= \frac{40}{3667} = 10.91 \times 10^{-3} \ \text{A}$$

Voltage across parallel combination,

$$V = IR$$
$$= 10.91 \times 10^{-3} \times 1667$$
$$= 18.18 \ \text{V}$$

This will be the voltmeter reading.
(b) For the parallel combination,

$$\frac{1}{R} = \frac{1}{R_1} + \frac{1}{R_2}$$
$$= \frac{1}{10^6} + \frac{1}{2 \times 10^3}$$
$$= \frac{1 + 500}{10^6} = \frac{501}{10^6}$$
$$R = \frac{10^6}{501} = 1996 \ \Omega$$

Total resistance of circuit,

$$R = R_1 + R_2$$
$$= 1996 + 2000$$
$$= 3996 \ \Omega$$

Current from battery,

$$I = \frac{V}{R}$$
$$= \frac{40}{3996} = 10.01 \times 10^{-3} \ \text{A}$$

Voltage across parallel combination (i.e., voltmeter reading),

$$V = IR$$
$$= 10.01 \times 10^{-3} \times 1996$$
$$= 19.98 \text{ V}$$

3. A meter movement gives f.s.d. for a current of 1 mA and its resistance is 10 Ω. What shunt resistor should be used to give a range of (a) 0–50 mA, (b) 0–5 A?

The circuit is shown in Fig. 8.6.
(a) For a total current of 50 mA, 1 mA is to flow through the meter movement while 49 mA flows through the shunt.
Voltage across meter movement,

$$V = IR$$
$$= 10^{-3} \times 10$$
$$= 10^{-2} \text{ V}$$

This is also the voltage across the shunt, hence shunt resistance,

$$R = \frac{V}{I}$$

$$= \frac{10^{-2}}{49 \times 10^{-3}} = 0.204 \text{ Ω}$$

(b) As before, voltage across meter movement is to be 10^{-2} V but now shunt current is $(5 \text{ A} - 1 \text{ mA}) = 4.999$ A.
Shunt resistance,

$$R = \frac{V}{I}$$

$$= \frac{10^{-2}}{4.999} = 0.002\ 000\ 4 \text{ Ω}$$

4. A meter movement gives f.s.d. for a current of 200 μA and has a resistance of 50 Ω. What multiplier resistor is required if it is to read (a) 0–10 V, (b) 0–200 V?

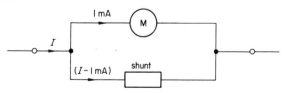

Figure 8.6

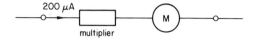

Figure 8.7

The circuit is shown in Fig. 8.7.
(a) Total circuit resistance,

$$R = \frac{V}{I}$$

$$= \frac{10}{200 \times 10^{-6}} = 50\ 000\ \Omega$$

$$R = R_1 + R_2$$

Hence resistance of multiplier is $50\ 000 - 50 = 49\ 950\ \Omega$ or $49.95\ k\Omega$
(b) Total circuit resistance,

$$R = \frac{V}{I}$$

$$= \frac{200}{200 \times 10^{-6}} = 10^6\ \Omega$$

Resistance of multiplier $= 10^6 - 50$

$$= 999\ 950\ \Omega \text{ or } 999.95\ k\Omega$$

5. A meter movement of resistance $20\ \Omega$ and giving f.s.d. for a current of $300\ \mu A$ is to be used as an ohm-meter. (a) What series resistor should be used in conjunction with a 1.5 V battery? (b) If, when a resistor is connected across the meter terminals, the instrument shows $\frac{1}{4}$ f.s.d., what resistance is being indicated?

(a) With meter terminals short-circuited, the meter is to give f.s.d., that is, current is to be $300\ \mu A$.
Total resistance,

$$R = \frac{V}{I}$$

$$= \frac{1.5}{300 \times 10^{-6}} = 5000\ \Omega$$

Hence, series resistor required is $(5000 - 20) = 4980\ \Omega$ or $4.98\ k\Omega$.

(b) The circuit is now as shown in Fig. 8.8. For $\frac{1}{4}$ f.s.d., meter current is $\frac{1}{4} \times 300 = 75\ \mu A$.

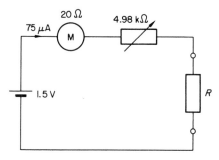

Figure 8.8

Resistance of whole circuit,

$$R = \frac{V}{I}$$

$$= \frac{1.5}{75 \times 10^{-6}} = 20\,000\ \Omega$$

Hence, external resistance,

$$R = 20\,000 - (4980 + 20)$$
$$= 15\,000\ \Omega \text{ or } 15\ k\Omega$$

8.6 Digital instruments

Increasing use is being made of 'digital instruments' in which the current, voltage, or resistance being measured is indicated not by a pointer and scale but directly in numerical form. Their operation resembles that of moving-coil instruments in that they make use of shunts and multipliers, but in place of the meter movement they have an 'analogue-to-digital converter'. This is an electronic circuit which converts the measured quantity into digital form so that it can be displayed as a number; usually by light-emitting diodes (l.e.d.) giving illuminated red numbers on a black background or by a liquid crystal display (l.c.d.) giving black numbers on a white background.

Digital instruments are available both as single-purpose instruments (usually voltmeters) and as multimeters. The advantages to the user are that they are easy to read and give minimal interference with the circuit under test – digital voltmeters, for example, have very high input resistance. From the point of view of the manufacturer, they include complicated electronic circuits but contain no moving parts – there is no delicate meter movement requiring skilled

assembly – and, since 'integrated circuits' are relatively easy to produce, it is to be expected that they will become increasingly com-
petitive as production techniques improve.

8.7 The cathode ray oscilloscope

This instrument makes use of the fact that an electron is charged
negatively so that it is attracted by a positively charged object and
repelled by a negatively charged one. Figure 8.9 shows a diagram of
a cathode ray tube. This is an evacuated glass tube containing at one
end the 'electron gun' which consists basically of a heated electrode
called the cathode, maintained at a high negative voltage relative to
the screen at the other end. This emits a stream of electrons (the
'cathode ray' from which the instrument takes its name) which is
attracted towards the positively charged screen. This 'electron beam'
travels first through the 'grid' which is charged negatively and is
used to control the number of electrons in the beam by repelling
some of them back towards the cathode. The beam then travels
through the 'focusing system' which, in this case, consists of two
further electrodes; by adjusting the voltages on these the electrons
may be made to converge so that all reach the screen within a small
area. The screen is coated with a 'phosphor', a substance which
gives off light when electrons strike it, so that a small, bright spot of
light is produced; the brightness can be varied by using the grid to
allow more or less electrons to flow.

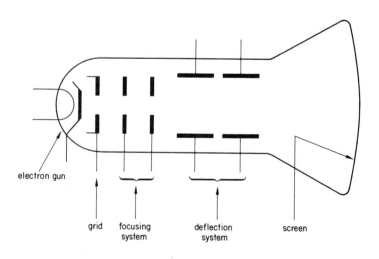

electron gun

grid | focusing | deflection | screen
system | system

Figure 8.9

Between the focusing system and the screen is the 'deflection system', consisting of a pair of plates arranged either side of the electron beam, followed by another pair at right angles to the first. Voltages are applied to these plates and if, for example, one of a pair is made positive and the other negative, electrons passing through will be attracted to one plate and repelled by the other so that they will have, in addition to their longitudinal motion, a lateral motion and will arrive at a different place on the screen, i.e., the beam will be 'deflected'. One pair of plates will deflect the beam horizontally (and is called the 'X-plates') while the other pair (the 'Y-plates') deflects the beam vertically.

Thus, when no voltage is applied to the deflection plates, the tube will display a single bright spot at the centre of its screen. On applying a voltage to the X-plates, this spot will move horizontally. A common feature of a cathode ray oscilloscope or C.R.O. (i.e., an instrument containing a cathode ray tube together with amplifiers, etc.) is the 'time base'. This is a circuit applying a voltage to the X-plates which increases steadily to a maximum then returns quickly to zero. This process is repeated (usually many times per second) and its effect is to 'sweep' the spot across the screen from left to right repeatedly; at all but slow speeds this will be seen as a continuous horizontal line which, by applying an additional 'shift' voltage to the plates, can be centralized on the screen as shown in Fig. 8.10(a). If now an alternating voltage is applied to the Y-plates, the spot will be given a vertical motion in addition to its horizontal motion. Since its vertical deflection will be proportional to the applied voltage and its horizontal motion is at constant velocity, the effect will be to draw a graph where $y =$ applied voltage and $x =$ time. If the time base frequency is the same as that of the applied voltage the same curve will be drawn repeatedly and it will appear as a continuous, steady trace. For a sinusoidal voltage (see Section 9.9) the display will appear as shown in Fig. 8.10(b).

The principal use of the C.R.O. is, in fact, in the examination of alternating signals; but its simplest application is the direct measurement of voltage. Since the deflection of the spot is proportional to the voltage applied to the deflection plates, a d.c. voltage can be measured by applying it to one pair of plates and measuring the resulting displacement of the spot. This method has the considerable advantage that since the plates are insulated from each other, the instrument will take no current and the circuit under test will be completely unaffected. An a.c. voltage will produce a line trace which can be measured; this length will, in fact, indicate $2 \times$ peak value. (In this case, an alternating current will flow since the plates

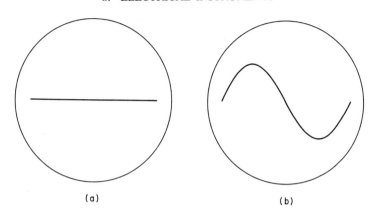

(a)   (b)

Figure 8.10

form a small capacitor; but, except at high frequencies, this current will be negligible.)

In the previous paragraph, it has been assumed that the voltage to be measured is applied directly to the deflection plates; but usually a commercial C.R.O. will not make provision for this. The deflection system is relatively insensitive – tens of volts are required to give a reasonable deflection–so that a C.R.O. is always provided with amplifiers and the input signal will be fed to one of these. In practice, therefore, the current taken by a C.R.O. from a voltage source will be that taken by its amplifier input–very small, but not zero.

The commercial C.R.O. thus contains facilities other than the cathode ray tube and its supplies, and the principal controls are as follows:

(1) 'Brightness' and 'focus' (operating as previously described).
(2) 'X shift' and 'Y shift': these impose an additional steady voltage on the deflection plates concerned, and their effect is to alter the position of the trace on the screen.
(3) X and Y amplifier gain controls (allowing for a wide range of input signal voltages).
(4) Time base speed: this controls the speed at which the spot sweeps across the screen.
(5) Time base 'trigger': this initiates the time base sweep at a fixed point in the signal cycle so that the trace appears stationary on the screen.

Problems

1. A battery of terminal voltage 12 V is connected to a circuit of total resistance 3 Ω. Find: (a) the current flowing; (b) the current

which would be shown by an ammeter of resistance 0.07 Ω inserted in the circuit.

(*Answer.* (a) 4 A (b) 3.91 A.)

2. A 6 kΩ resistor is connected in series with a 4 kΩ resistor across a 200 V supply. Find: (a) the voltage across the 6 kΩ resistor; (b) the reading which would be shown by a voltmeter of resistance 100 kΩ connected across it.

(*Answer.* (a) 120 V (b) 117.2 V.)

3. A 9 V battery is connected to two 50 kΩ resistors arranged in series. What potential difference would be indicated by a voltmeter of resistance (a) 10 kΩ (b) 1 MΩ connected across one of them?

(*Answer.* (a) 1.29 V (b) 4.39 V.)

4. A battery has an e.m.f. of 9 V and its internal resistance is 80 Ω. What would be the reading of a voltmeter of resistance 10 kΩ connected across its terminals?

(*Answer.* 8.93 V.)

5. A meter movement has a resistance of 10 Ω and gives f.s.d. for a current of 500 μA. What current will give f.s.d. when a 1 Ω resistor is connected in parallel with the movement?

(*Answer.* 5.5 mA.)

6. A meter movement of resistance 10 Ω giving f.s.d. for a current of 2 mA is to be used as an ammeter reading 0–5 A. Show how this would be done and calculate the value of the resistor required.

(*Answer.* 0.004 002 Ω.)

7. A meter movement has a resistance of 12 Ω and gives f.s.d for a current of 400 μA. What shunt resistor is required if it is to be used as an ammeter with a range of (a) 0–50 mA, (b) 0–1 A?

(*Answer.* (a) 0.096 77 Ω (b) 0.004 802 Ω.)

8. A meter movement has a resistance of 50 Ω and gives f.s.d. for a currrent of 100 μA. What shunt resistor is required if it is to be used as a milliammeter with a range of (a) 0–1 mA (b) 0–10 mA?

(*Answer.* (a) 5.556 Ω (b) 0.5051 Ω)

9. A meter movement has a resistance of 10 Ω and gives f.s.d. for a current of 5 mA. What shunt resistor is required if it is to be used as an ammeter reading 0–500 A?

(*Answer.* 10^{-4} Ω.)

10. A meter movement having a resistance of $30\,\Omega$ and giving f.s.d. for a current of $200\,\mu\text{A}$ is to be used as a voltmeter reading 0–50 V. Show how this would be done and calculate the value of the resistor required.

(*Answer.* 249.97 kΩ.)

11. A meter movement giving f.s.d. for a current of 1 mA and having a resistance of $10\,\Omega$ is to be used as a voltmeter having a range (a) 0–5 V, (b) 0–30 V. What series resistor is required in each case?

(*Answer.* 4.99 kΩ (b) 29.99 kΩ.)

12. A meter movement gives f.s.d. for a current of $50\,\mu\text{A}$ and has a resistance of $50\,\Omega$. What series resistor is required if it is to be used as a voltmeter reading (a) 0–5 V, (b) 0–200 V?

(*Answer.* (a) 99.95 kΩ (b) 4 MΩ.)

13. A voltmeter reads 0–250 V and has a total resistance of $1\,\text{M}\Omega$. It is desired to extend its range to 0–1000 V by using an external resistor. Show how this would be done and calculate the value of the required resistor.

(*Answer.* 3 MΩ.)

14. A meter movement has a resistance of $40\,\Omega$ and gives f.s.d. for a current of $150\,\mu\text{A}$. It is to be used as an ohm-meter operated by a 9 V battery. Show how this would be done, and state the value of the resistor required. If an external resistor is now connected across the ohm-meter terminals and the pointer moves to $\frac{1}{3}$ f.s.d., what resistance is being indicated?

(*Answer.* 59.96 kΩ, 120 kΩ.)

15. A battery of e.m.f. 45 V is connected to the Y-plates of a cathode ray tube and the spot is deflected 21 mm. An alternating voltage is now applied to the Y-plates and a vertical line 63 mm long is obtained. What is the peak value of the alternating voltage?

(*Answer.* 67.5 V.)

9. Electricity and magnetism

9.1 Force on a conductor in a magnetic field

Surrounding a bar magnet, or a coil of wire through which a current is being passed there is a region in which, although nothing is visible, various effects are observed; this is referred to as a 'magnetic field'. The direction of the field at any point may be found using a small, pivoted, magnetized needle (often called a 'compass needle') which will align itself with the direction of the field. Using such a device 'lines of magnetic flux' may be plotted and Figs 9.1(a) and 9.1(b) show these for a bar magnet and for a 'solenoid' (i.e., a coil of wire of appreciable length compared with its diameter): the direction of any line being considered as proceeding from a north pole to a south pole. (These patterns may also be shown by placing a piece of paper over, for example, a bar magnet and sprinkling iron filings over it.)

It will be seen that in the case of the solenoid, the lines form closed paths and this is in fact true also of the bar magnet – the lines of flux pass through the metal of the magnet. Thus for every magnetic circuit there is a total amount of 'magnetic flux'. The unit of magnetic flux is the weber (Wb) and it is referred to by the symbol ϕ. For a definition of the weber we must consider the effect of electromagnetic induction (see Section 9.5): the weber is defined as the amount of flux which, linked with a coil of one turn, produces an e.m.f. of one volt when reduced to zero in one second.

It will also be seen that within the solenoid the lines of force are much closer to each other than they are externally; the same total amount of flux is present but within the solenoid it passes through a much smaller area. Another way of describing this difference would be to say that there is a greater *flux density* within the solenoid. The unit of flux density is the tesla (T) and it is referred to by the symbol B. Flux density is conveniently thought of as 'lines of flux per unit cross-sectional area', so that the definition of the tesla is a density of

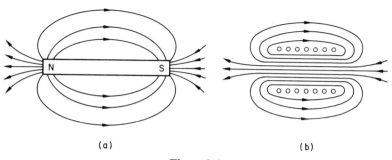

(a)   (b)

Figure 9.1

1 weber of flux per square metre of cross-sectional area and, in general,

$$B = \frac{\phi}{A} \tag{9.1}$$

If a current is passed through a conductor, a magnetic field is created whose lines of flux form concentric circles round the conductor. Figure 9.2 shows this for a conductor which is at right angles to the paper and in which current is flowing into the paper. The direction of the lines of flux may be found using the 'right-hand screw rule' – if a right-handed screw is turned so that it progresses in the direction of the current, its direction of rotation will show the direction of the lines of flux. If such a conductor is placed in a magnetic field and at right angles to this field, the interaction of this field with that of the conductor will produce a force tending to move the conductor as in Fig. 9.3. The direction of this force will be prependicular both to the conductor and to the magnetic field and may be found using 'Fleming's left-hand rule' – if the thumb,

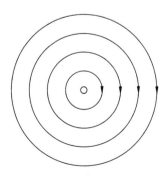

Figure 9.2

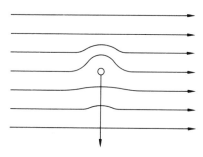

Figure 9.3

forefinger, and second finger of the left hand are extended (as in Fig. 9.4), then placed so that the forefinger points in the direction of the magnetic flux and the second finger in the direction of current flow, the thumb will indicate the direction of motion.

The magnitude of the force produced may be expected to increase with increasing flux density B, with increasing current I, and with greater length of conductor l. It is found, in fact, to depend on the product of these three quantities and, provided SI units are used, this product will give the force in newtons:

$$F = BIl \qquad (9.2)$$

If, instead of a single conductor, a rectangular coil is placed in a magnetic field so that the conductors forming two of its sides are at right angles to the field, forces will act in the directions shown in Fig. 9.5. This figure shows a cross-sectional view of such an arrange-

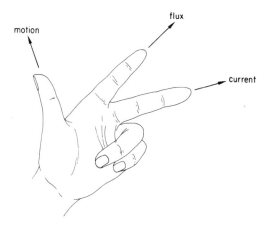

Figure 9.4

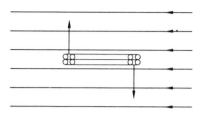

Figure 9.5

ment and it is assumed that the current passes round the coil so that in all conductors on the left-hand side the direction of the current is into the paper while for all those on the right-hand side the current flows out of the paper. (It should be noted that the other two sides of the coil will experience no forces since their conductors are in line with the magnetic field.) It will be seen that the forces form a couple, i.e., the tendency is to rotate the coil clockwise.

Worked examples

1. A solenoid encloses a cylinder of diameter 50 mm and the total flux passing through this area is 2.5 mWb. What is the flux density?

From Eq. 9.1,

$$B = \frac{\phi}{A}$$

Here

$$\phi = 2.5 \times 10^{-3} \, \text{Wb}$$

and

$$A = \pi \times (25 \times 10^{-3})^2$$
$$= 1.963 \times 10^{-3} \, \text{m}^2$$

Hence

$$B = \frac{2.5 \times 10^{-3}}{1.963 \times 10^{-3}} = 1.273 \, \text{T}$$

2. Figure 9.6 shows a conductor placed at right angles to the magnetic field between two bar magnets. If a current is passed in the direction shown, in which direction will the conductor tend to move? If the flux density is 2 T, the length of the conductor 20 mm, and the current 30 A, what will be the force on the conductor?

The direction of the magnetic field will be from the north pole to

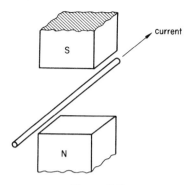

Figure 9.6

the south pole, i.e., vertically upwards. Applying Fleming's left-hand rule, the direction of motion would be horizontally and to the right.

From Eq. 9.2,

$$F = BIl$$
$$= 2 \times 30 \times (20 \times 10^{-3})$$
$$= 1.2 \text{ N}$$

3. A rectangular coil measuring $100 \text{ mm} \times 100 \text{ mm}$ is placed in a magnetic field of flux density 0.5 T so that two of its sides are at right angles to the field (as in Fig. 9.4). If the coil consists of 20 turns and the current in it is 2 A, what will be the turning moment produced?

For each conductor,

$$F = BIl$$
$$= 0.5 \times 2 \times 0.1$$
$$= 0.1 \text{ N}$$

There are 20 conductors on each side of the coil, so that on each side the force produced is $(20 \times 0.1) = 2 \text{ N}$. These forces are separated by a distance of 0.1 m, hence they form a couple whose turning moment is $(2 \times 0.1) = 0.2 \text{ N m}$.

9.2 The moving-coil instrument

This instrument is based on the fact (described at the end of Section 9.1) that a rectangular coil through which a current is being passed, suitably placed in a magnetic field, experiences a turning moment. Figure 9.7 shows the basic construction of such a meter movement; the magnetic field is provided by a permanent magnet and the shape of its poles, together with the use of a cylindrical soft-iron core, give a radial magnetic field of uniform intensity over the regions through

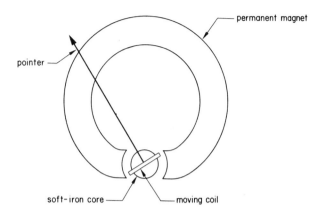

Figure 9.7

which the active sides of the coil travel. On passing a current through the coil, a turning moment is produced which is resisted by two spiral springs; these are not shown in the diagram but are placed around the pivots at each end of the coil and are also used to carry the current into and out of the coil. The coil (to which the pointer is attached) will rotate until the turning moment due to the current passing through it is equalled by the restraining action of the springs; and since the restoring moment of the springs increases in direct proportion to the rotation of the coil, it follows that the pointer movement will be directly proportional to the current in the coil. Thus the instrument has a linear scale.

The sensitivity of the instrument depends on the number of turns in the moving coil, the flux density produced by the magnet, and the stiffness of the springs. By using a coil of many turns, a powerful magnet, and light springs, the movement may be made to operate on very small currents; a typical movement will give full-scale deflection for a current of $100 \, \mu A$ (see Section 8.1).

One major disadvantage of this meter movement is that it is suitable for direct current only. If the direction of the current in the coil is reversed, the forces on its conductors will also be reversed so that if an alternating current is passed through the coil it will attempt to move alternately forwards and backwards and will, in fact, oscillate about its zero position.

9.3 The d.c. motor

The fact that a rectangular coil through which a current is being passed, suitably positioned in a magnetic field, experiences a turning moment (see Section 9.1) can, as described in Section 9.2, be used in the moving-coil meter movement. It can also be used in the construction of a simple d.c. motor. If such a coil (as in Fig. 9.5) is unrestrained, it will rotate until it reaches a vertical position; the forces on the conductors will now be in line with the pivot, and the coil will no longer experience a turning moment. If, however, the current in the coil is reversed (and the coil given a slight further rotation – which in fact would occur due to the inertia of the coil), it will now experience a turning moment in the same direction as previously and will rotate through a further 180°. This reversal of current can be arranged using a device called a 'commutator'. Figure 9.8 shows such an arrangement (using a single-turn coil) in which the commutator consists of a split ring (whose halves are insulated from each other) making contact with 'brushes' which convey current from a battery. It will be seen that each time the coil reaches a vertical position, the current through it will be reversed so that the coil will rotate continuously – in other words, the device functions as a simplified d.c. motor.

9.4   The moving-iron instrument

The principle of operation of a moving-iron instrument is shown in Fig. 9.9. There are two soft-iron bars (one fixed and one movable)

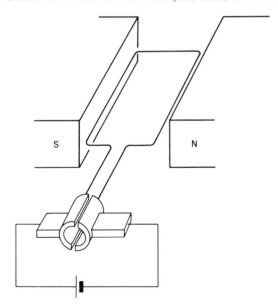

Figure 9.8

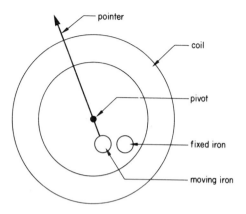

Figure 9.9

placed within a coil of wire through which the current to be measured is passed. The magnetic field produced by this current will magnetize both the iron bars, and they will both be magnetized in the same direction so that similar poles will be produced at their ends. Since like poles repel each other, the movable bar will tend to move away from the fixed bar, causing its attached pointer to move over the scale. This motion is resisted by a spiral spring (not shown on the diagram) and the pointer will come to rest when the restoring moment of the spring equals the turning moment due to the repulsion of the moving iron by the fixed one.

The motion of the pointer will not be in direct proportion to the current passed through the coil so that, unlike the moving-coil instrument, the moving-iron instrument will not have a linear scale. It will also require a much larger current for its operation. It does, however, have the advantage that it will measure both direct and alternating currents; if the current in the coil is reversed, the direction of magnetization of both the iron bars will also be reversed but they will still have similar poles at their ends, so that for either direction of current the bars repel each other.

9.5 Electromagnetic induction

An e.m.f. is induced in any conductor placed within a magnetic field if the flux 'linked' with the conductor varies. This variation may be caused in two ways; the conductor may be moved, so that it 'cuts through' the lines of magnetic flux, or the conductor may remain stationary while the magnetic flux varies. Figure 9.10 shows a simple way of demonstrating electromagnetic induction. A bar magnet is

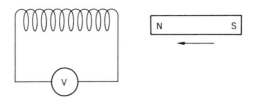

Figure 9.10

moved into a coil of wire to which a sensitive voltmeter is connected, and it will be observed that while the magnet is in motion, the voltmeter shows the presence of an e.m.f. in the coil. While the magnet is stationary in the coil, the voltmeter will read zero and when the magnet is moved in the opposite direction (i.e., out of the coil) the voltmeter will be deflected in the opposite direction. Thus, it is seen that it is only when the 'flux linkages' are being changed that the e.m.f. is produced; it may also be observed that the faster the magnet is moved, the greater the e.m.f. produced. Furthermore, an experiment performed using the same magnet but a coil consisting of more turns would show that for more turns and the same speed of movement of the magnet an increased e.m.f. is produced.

The e.m.f. is in fact proportional to the *rate of change* of flux linkages and provided SI units are used for all quantities, the e.m.f. (in volts) will be equal to the product of the number of turns and the rate of change of magnetic flux (in Wb/s). Thus if the flux linked with a coil of N turns changes at a steady rate from ϕ_1 to ϕ_2 in t seconds, the e.m.f. produced will be given by

$$E = N\frac{(\phi_2 - \phi_1)}{t} \qquad (9.3)$$

It is possible to forecast the direction of the e.m.f. produced in the above experiment and this may be done in two ways; by applying 'Fleming's right-hand rule' or by using 'Lenz's law'. Fleming's right-hand rule applies to a single conductor moving relative to a magnetic field, and states that if the thumb, forefinger, and second finger of the right hand are extended (as in Fig. 9.11), then placed so that the forefinger points in the direction of the magnetic flux and the thumb in the direction in which the conductor moves relative to the magnetic field, the second finger will point in the direction of the induced e.m.f.

Lenz's law states that whenever an e.m.f. is induced, the resulting current is always in such a direction as to *oppose* whatever is creating the e.m.f. Thus, referring to Fig. 9.10, the current induced

181

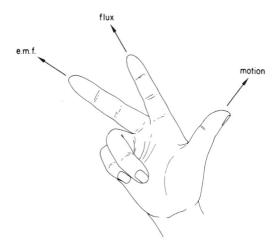

Figure 9.11

in the coil would produce a magnetic field which would oppose the motion of the bar magnet – the field of the coil would be similar to that of a bar magnet having a north pole at its right-hand end so that the bar magnet would be repelled. This law follows from the principle of conversation of energy; the coil is producing an output of electrical energy and this must be balanced by an input of mechanical energy to the bar magnet – it must experience an opposing force so that work is done in pushing it into the coil.

9.6 Self induction

As illustrated in Fig. 9.1(b), whenever a current is passed through a coil of wire, a magnetic field is produced. Suppose this current is to be increased; this will result in a larger amount of magnetic flux. This flux is, however, 'linked' with the coil so that there will be an increase in the amount of 'flux linkages' and, as stated in Section 9.5, this must result in the creation of an e.m.f. By Lenz's law, this e.m.f. will oppose the effect creating it – it will be in opposition to the change in current and is called a 'back e.m.f.'. This effect is called 'self induction' and the coil would be said to form part of an 'inductive circuit'.

Furthermore, since the e.m.f. produced is proportional to the rate of change of flux linkages, it will be proportional to the *rate of change* of the current in the coil. Thus any attempt to change the current in an inductive circuit will result in the creation of 'back e.m.f.' and, if the current is altered rapidly, this e.m.f. will be large.

This is particularly noticeable when an attempt is made to 'switch off' an inductive circuit. As the switch is opened, the current decreases rapidly to zero and this creates a large e.m.f. which, in effect, attempts to keep the current flowing and results in an arc across the switch contacts.

9.7 Mutual induction

If two coils are linked with the same magnetic circuit (as would be the case if one was wound over the other) and the current in one coil is changed, this will change the flux linked with *both* coils so that, in addition to the 'back e.m.f.' produced in the first coil, an e.m.f. will be created in the other coil. This phenomenon is called 'mutual induction'. The e.m.f. produced in the second coil will depend on the number of turns of this coil and thus may be smaller or larger than the back e.m.f. of the first coil.

9.8 The transformer

Use is made of mutual induction in the construction of a *transformer*. This consists of a magnetic circuit of soft iron (usually in the form of a number of thin plates or 'laminations') on which are wound two coils – the 'primary coil' and the 'secondary coil'. Figure 9.12(a) shows one possible arrangement and Fig. 9.12(b) gives the symbol used to represent a transformer.

An alternating voltage is applied to the 'primary coil' and a small alternating current flows. This produces an alternating flux in the magnetic circuit which is just sufficient to induce a back e.m.f. in the primary coil equal to the applied voltage. Since this alternating flux

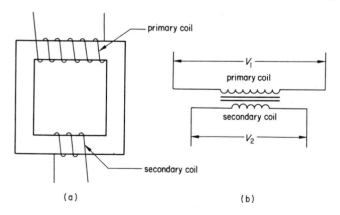

(a)   (b)

Figure 9.12

is also linked with the secondary coil, an alternating e.m.f. is induced in this coil; and since the same flux links with both coils it follows that the e.m.f. in each will be proportional to the number of turns. The e.m.f. of the primary coil is, as stated above, equal to the supply voltage; thus the ratio of the voltage output of the secondary coil to the supply voltage will be the ratio of the number of turns:

$$\frac{V_2}{V_1} = \frac{N_2}{N_1} \tag{9.4}$$

i.e., the voltage ratio is equal to the turns ratio.

If the secondary coil of a transformer is connected to an external circuit (say, a resistor) a current will flow and there will be a corresponding flow of current in the primary coil. The ratio of these currents may be found using the principle of conservation of energy, since in the transformer itself there is very little loss of energy. Thus power taken from secondary coil = power supplied to primary coil. For a purely resistive a.c. circuit, power is equal to the product of voltage and current, so that

$$V_2 I_2 = V_1 I_1$$

hence

$$\frac{I_2}{I_1} = \frac{V_1}{V_2}$$

But from Eq. 9.4,

$$\frac{V_1}{V_2} = \frac{N_1}{N_2}$$

hence

$$\frac{I_2}{I_1} = \frac{N_1}{N_2} \tag{9.5}$$

i.e., the current ratio is equal to the turns ratio.

Worked examples

4. A single conductor is moved so that the flux linked with it changes from 5 mWb to 10 mWb in 0.1 s. What will be the induced e.m.f. (assuming the rate of change of flux to be constant)?

From Eq. 9.3,

$$E = N\frac{(\phi_2 - \phi_1)}{t}$$

Here

$$N = 1$$
$$(\phi_2 - \phi_1) = (10 - 5)\,\text{mWb} = 5\,\text{mWb or } 0.005\,\text{Wb}$$

and

$$t = 0.1\,\text{s}$$

hence

$$E = 1 \times \frac{0.005}{0.1}$$
$$= 0.05\,\text{V}$$

5. The flux linked with a 200-turn coil changes (at a steady rate) from 1 mWb to 5 mWb in 0.1 s. What will be the induced e.m.f.?

From Eq. 9.3,

$$E = N\frac{(\phi_2 - \phi_1)}{t}$$
$$= 200 \times \frac{(0.005 - 0.001)}{0.1}$$
$$= 8\,\text{V}$$

6. A 500-turn coil carries a current which produces a magnetic flux of 4 mWb. If this current is reduced to zero in 0.05 s, what will be the back e.m.f. due to self induction?

If the current is reduced to zero, the magnetic flux will also be reduced to zero. Hence, applying Eq. 9.3,

$$E = N\frac{(\phi_2 - \phi_1)}{t}$$
$$= 500 \times \frac{(0 - 0.004)}{0.05}$$
$$= -40\,\text{V}$$

i.e., a back e.m.f. of 40 V would be produced.

7. The primary coil of a transformer has 500 turns and the secondary coil 100 turns. If a 240 V a.c. supply is connected to the primary coil, what will be the output voltage? If a current of 10 A is taken from the secondary coil, what will be the current taken from the supply?

Output voltage: from Eq. 9.4,

$$\frac{V_2}{V_1} = \frac{N_2}{N_1}$$

Hence

$$V_2 = V_1 \times \frac{N_2}{N_1}$$

$$= 240 \times \frac{100}{500}$$

$$= 48\ V$$

Input current: from Eq. 9.5,

$$\frac{I_2}{I_1} = \frac{N_1}{N_2}$$

hence

$$I_1 = I_2 \times \frac{N_2}{N_1}$$

$$= 10 \times \frac{100}{500}$$

$$= 2\ A$$

9.9 The simple generator

Figure 9.13 shows an a.c. generator in its simplest form. A conductor in the form of a single rectangular loop is rotated in the uniform magnetic field between the poles of two permanent magnets. Its ends are connected to two 'slip rings' so that while the coil is rotated, current can pass to and from it via the slip rings and two stationary 'brushes' which are connected to an external circuit.

In the position shown, the active sides of the loop are cutting the magnetic flux and an e.m.f. will be generated which will cause a current to flow in the external circuit. As the loop rotates, the rate at which the conductors cut the flux will decrease until the loop has rotated through 90°.The conductors will now be moving parallel to the magnetic field so that no e.m.f. is generated. Further rotation of the loop will cause the conductors to cut the flux at an increasing rate so that the e.m.f. will increase, reaching a maximum when the loop has rotated through a further 90°. This e.m.f. will, however, be in the opposite direction since the conductors are moving in the opposite direction relative to the flux. If the e.m.f. is plotted against

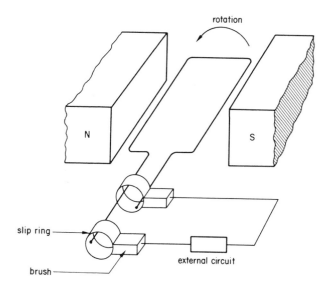

Figure 9.13

angle of rotation (commencing at a time when the conductors are moving parallel to the flux, i.e., at a point of zero e.m.f.) a graph similar to Fig. 9.14 will be produced.

This shape may be recognized as similar to that of a graph of $\sin \phi$ against ϕ; in fact the waveform (i.e., the shape of the graph of e.m.f. or current against time) is described as 'sinusoidal' and the 'instantaneous' value of the e.m.f. (i.e., its value at any particular moment and here given the symbol e) is in fact given by

$$e = E_p \sin \theta \qquad (9.6)$$

where E_p is the 'peak value' of the e.m.f. The current in the external circuit thus passes alternately forwards and backwards, hence the

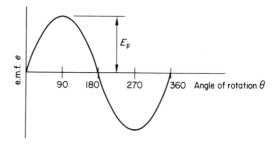

Figure 9.14

term 'alternating current' (usually abbreviated to a.c.). If the external circuit is a purely resistive one, the instantaneous current i will be given by e/R, where R is the resistance of the circuit. Thus the current waveform is, like that of the e.m.f., sinusoidal, and

$$i = I_p \sin \theta \tag{9.7}$$

where I_p is the maximum or 'peak value' of the current.

9.10 Alternating current

In order to describe an a.c. voltage or current, two characteristics must be stated; its *frequency* and its *magnitude*. Frequency is defined as the number of times the voltage or current goes through a complete cycle (corresponding to one revolution of the loop in Fig. 9.13) per second, and is measured in hertz (Hz); thus,

frequency in Hz = number of cycles per second

The frequency of both domestic and industrial supplies is 50 Hz so that in this case both voltage and current pass through 50 complete cycles every second.

The magnitude of an a.c. quantity could be given by stating its peak value but this is not normally done. The domestic supply voltage, for example, is stated as 240 V but it must be pointed out that this not the peak value; it is the value of a d.c. voltage which would give the same heating effect (i.e., power consumption) when applied to a resistor, and is called the root-mean-square or r.m.s. value. The theoretical derivation of this quantity relies on the fact that, for an instantaneous current i, the power consumed by a resistor is i^2R (see Section 4.8) and it may be shown that, provided the waveform is sinusoidal.

$$I_{r.m.s.} = \frac{I_p}{\sqrt{2}} = 0.7071 I_p \tag{9.8}$$

also

$$V_{r.m.s.} = \frac{V_p}{\sqrt{2}} = 0.7071 V_p \tag{9.9}$$

9.11 Single- and three-phase supplies

Domestic consumers are usually supplied with the kind of alternating current described in Section 9.9 (i.e., one involving two conductors only) and this is referred to as a 'single-phase' supply. For

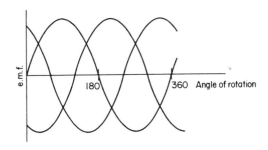

Figure 9.15

industrial consumers, however, this kind of supply suffers from the serious disadvantage that (for technical reasons beyond the scope of this book) it is unsuitable for all but the smallest electric motors; such consumers are normally given a three-phase supply.

A simple generator for such a supply would be similar in construction to that shown in Fig. 9.13 but with three rectangular loops equally spaced (i.e., at 120° to each other). This would produce three alternating outputs as shown in Fig. 9.15. All major power supply generators are constructed on this principle and all power supplies are of this form.

The secondary windings of a power supply transformer would normally be arranged in 'star connection' so that the supply involves four conductors – three 'lines' and a 'neutral'; domestic consumers requiring a single-phase supply would be connected between one line and neutral as shown in Fig. 9.16. An electric motor used by an industrial consumer would probably have its windings arranged in 'delta connection' as shown by Fig. 9.17. It may be shown that 'line voltage' (i.e., that between any two line conductors) is related to

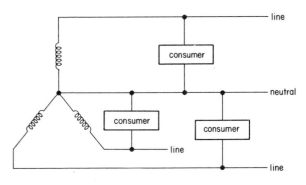

Figure 9.16

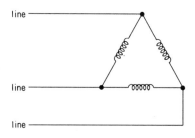

Figure 9.17

'phase voltage' (i.e., that between one line conductor and the neutral conductor) by the factor $\sqrt{3}$ so that

$$\text{line voltage} = \text{phase voltage} \times \sqrt{3}$$
$$= \text{phase voltage} \times 1.732 \qquad (9.10)$$

Thus, if a supply cable is to feed both domestic and industrial consumers, the phase voltage would be made 240 V so that the line voltage would be $(240 \times 1.732) = 415$ V.

Worked examples

8. An alternating e.m.f. has a peak value of 100 V and a frequency of 50 Hz. What will be the instantaneous value of the e.m.f. 1 ms after it has passed through zero?

From Eq. 9.6,

$$e = E_p \sin \theta$$

Here, an angle of 360° would correspond to the time for one complete cycle, that is, 1/50 s or 20 ms. Thus, in this case,

$$\theta = 360 \times \frac{1}{20} = 18°$$

hence

$$e = 100 \sin 18°$$
$$= 30.9 \text{ V}$$

9. An alternating voltage has a peak value of 100 V. What is its r.m.s. value?

From Eq. 9.9,
$$V_{r.m.s.} = 0.707 V_p$$

hence in this case,

$$V_{r.m.s} = 0.7071 \times 100$$
$$= 70.71 \ V$$

10. An alternating current has an r.m.s. value of 15 A. What is its peak value?

From Eq. 9.8,

$$I_{r.m.s.} = \frac{I_p}{\sqrt{2}}$$

hence

$$I_p = I_{r.m.s.} \times \sqrt{2}$$
$$= 15 \times 1.414$$
$$= 21.21 \ A$$

11. The voltage between the lines of a three-phase supply is 500 V. What is the voltage between one line and the neutral conductor?

From Eq. 9.10,

$$\text{line voltage} = \text{phase voltage} \times 1.732$$

hence

$$\text{phase voltage} = \frac{\text{line voltage}}{1.732}$$
$$= \frac{500}{1.732}$$
$$= 288.7 \ V$$

Problems

1. A flux of 600 μWb passes through a cross-sectional area measuring 50 mm $\times$ 40 mm. What is the flux density?

(*Answer.* 0.3 T.)

2. The flux density of a magnetic field is 2.5 T. What total flux would there be in an area of circular cross-section of diameter 50 mm?

(*Answer.* 4.91 mWb.)

3. A conductor is at right angles to the paper and current flows

out of the paper. Sketch the magnetic field surrounding the conductor and state the direction of the lines of flux.

(*Answer.* Anticlockwise.)

4. A magnetic field is in the plane of the paper and the direction of its lines of flux is from left to right. A conductor is placed in the plane of the paper at right angles to this field and it carries a current in a direction from the top of the page to the bottom. In which direction will it tend to move?

(*Answer.* Vertically upwards from the paper.)

5. A conductor 100 mm long is placed at right angles to a magnetic field of flux density 0.8 T. If the current is 5 A, what will be the force on the conductor?

(*Answer.* 0.4 N.)

6. A conductor 60 mm long is placed at right angles to a magnetic field. When a current of 20 A is passed through it a force of 1.8 N is produced. What is the flux density?

(*Answer.* 1.5 T.)

7. A rectangular coil consisting of 50 turns and measuring 60 mm × 60 mm is placed so that two of its sides are at right angles to a field of flux density 2 T. What turning moment will be produced when a current of 5 A is passed through the coil?

(*Answer.* 1.8 N m.)

8. A single conductor is moved so that the flux linked with it changes (at a steady rate) from 1 mWb to 10 mWb in 0.05 s. What will be the induced e.m.f.?

(*Answer.* 0.18 V.)

9. The flux linked with a 500-turn coil changes (at a steady rate) from 2 mWb to 10 mWb in 0.2 s. What will be the induced e.m.f.?

(*Answer.* 20 V.)

10. A 300-turn coil carries a current which produces a magnetic flux of 5 mWb. What back e.m.f. will be produced if this current is reduced to zero in 0.02 s?

(*Answer.* 75 V.)

11. The current in a 600-turn coil is increased so that the magnetic flux linked with the coil increases from 2 mWb to 4 mWb in 0.1 s. What will be the back e.m.f. due to self induction?

(*Answer.* 12 V.)

12. The primary coil of a transformer has 600 turns and the secondary coil 50 turns. If a 240 V a.c. supply is connected to the primary coil, what will be the voltage output of the secondary coil? If the primary coil takes a current of 1 A, what is the output current?

(*Answer.* 20 V, 12 A.)

13. A transformer is to give an output of 12 V when supplied at 240 V. If its primary coil has 1000 turns, how many turns should its secondary coil have?

(*Answer.* 50.)

14. A transformer has a primary coil of 200 turns and a secondary coil of 1000 turns. What will be its output voltage when supplied at 240 V, and what current will be taken from the supply when its output current is 0.5 A?

(*Answer.* 1200 V, 2.5 A.)

15. A transformer has a primary coil of 400 turns and a secondary coil of 80 turns. What current will be taken from a 200 V supply when a 20 Ω resistor is connected to its secondary coil?

(*Answer.* 0.4 A.)

16. An alternating e.m.f. has a peak value of 200 V and a frequency of 50 Hz. What will be its instantaneous value 2 ms after it has passed through zero?

(*Answer.* 117.6 V.)

17. An alternating current has a peak value of 15 A and a frequency of 50 Hz. What will be its instantaneous value 3 ms after it has passed through zero?

(*Answer.* 12.14 A.)

18. The r.m.s. value of the alternating voltage of a domestic supply is 240 V. What is its peak value?

(*Answer.* 339.4 V.)

19. An alternating current has a peak value of 25 A. What is its r.m.s. value?

(*Answer.* 17.68 A.)

20. In a three-phase supply system the voltage between one line and the neutral is 220 V. What is the voltage between the lines?

(*Answer.* 381 V.)

10. Heat

10.1 Heat and temperature

A simple description of temperature is 'a measure of hotness' – we are able to sense that an object is 'hot' or 'cold' by touching it. The question, 'What is temperature, i.e., what makes an object hot?' can only be answered by considering the individual atoms or molecules of which the object is composed. Although the object as a whole may be at rest, its molecules are, in fact, in motion – in the case of a solid, they are in a state of vibration – and the greater this motion, the higher the temperature. Since we cannot observe individual molecules, we measure temperature by observing one of its effects and the device used for this purpose is called a *thermometer*. For example, by making use of the effect of expansion we may construct the familiar liquid-in-glass thermometer and, by placing a series of marks on its stem, we may establish a *temperature scale*; the one in general use is the Celsius scale.

The word 'heat', as commonly used, has a variety of meanings and is, in fact, often confused with temperature; but in scientific and engineering applications it is defined as *energy in transit between two bodies because of a difference in temperature*. When a hot object is brought into contact with a cold one, the faster-moving molecules of the hot object impart some of their kinetic energy to the slower-moving molecules of the cold one, and this process will continue until both are at the same temperature; there is a *transfer of energy* and this is referred to as a *heat transfer* (symbol Q). It must be emphasized that heat, like work, cannot be stored and although the energy possessed by the molecules of a hot object is often thought of as 'stored heat' the correct term for this energy is in fact *internal energy* (U).

10.2 Expansion

One of the effects of a temperature increase is that, with a few exceptions, substances expand; as the vibration of the molecules increases, they tend to make more room for themselves. For a solid, this expansion will take place equally in all directions so that all

194

dimensions of a solid object will increase. (Conversely, for a decrease in temperature, the object will contract and all its dimensions will decrease.) The amount by which a dimension increases will obviously be proportional to the original dimension, and is also found to be directly proportional to the change in temperature, so that

expansion x = original dimension l × temperature change t

× a constant

This constant is called the *coefficient of linear expansion* (α).
  Thus,

$$x = \alpha l t \qquad (10.1)$$

For example, the coefficient of linear expansion of steel is 12×10^{-6} per °C, and this means that for every 1 °C rise in temperature, a bar of steel 1 m long would increase its length by 12×10^{-6} m (that is, 0.012 mm).

  Liquids do not have fixed dimensions – they will take up the shape of their container – but a given mass of liquid has a definite volume. Hence for liquids we are concerned with the change in volume produced by a temperature change. This is found to be directly proportional to the temperature change and to the original volume, so that

volumetric expansion v = original volume V

× temperature change t × a constant

The constant is called the *coefficient of volumetric expansion* (γ).
  Thus,

$$v = \gamma V t \qquad (10.2)$$

For example, the coefficient of volumetric expansion of mercury is 180×10^{-6} per °C, so that for every 1 °C rise in temperature, 1 litre of mercury would increase its volume by 180×10^{-6} or 0.000 18 litre (that is, 0.18 ml).

  It may be noted, that, in general, liquids expand more than solids for the same temperature rise. In a mercury-in-glass thermometer, for example, an increase in temperature causes an expansion of the glass bulb (increasing its volume) as well as an expansion of the mercury. The increase in volume of the mercury is, however, much greater than the increase in volume of the bulb so that the excess mercury is forced up the thermometer stem.

10.3 Heat capacity

As energy in the form of heat is transferred to an object, its molecular motion will increase so that its temperature will rise. The amount of energy transfer required to produce a given temperature rise will depend on the mass of the object and also on the material from which it is made. The energy required to produce unit rise in temperature (1 °C) for unit mass (1 kg) of a substance is called its *specific heat capacity* (*c*). For example, to raise the temperature of 1 kg of copper by 1 °C, a heat transfer of 385 J is required; thus the specific heat capacity of copper is 385 J/kg °C.

The amount of heat energy required to raise the temperature of a substance will obviously be greater for a larger mass. It will also be proportional to the change in temperature, so that

heat transfer = mass × specific heat capacity × temperature change

$$Q = mct \tag{10.3}$$

10.4 Changes of state

Matter can exist in three states: solid, liquid, and vapour or gas. (There is a slight distinction between the latter terms; 'vapour' is used to describe substances such as steam whose temperatures are near to their boiling points, while the term 'gas' is reserved for substances such as oxygen or air which are at temperatures so far above their boiling points that they cannot be liquefied by compression.) When a solid melts, or when a liquid boils, there is a *change of state* and this has two important characteristics:

(1) the change will require a transfer of heat energy to the substance (or, for a change in the reverse direction, heat energy will be given out by the substance); and
(2) the temperature of the substance will remain constant throughout the change.

The explanation for this is that heat energy transferred to the molecules of the substance is used not to increase their motion but to alter the molecular structure. The molecules of a solid, for example, are held firmly in place by forces of attraction, and energy is required to overcome these forces if the molecules are to have the mobility which will make the substance a liquid.

The temperature at which a substance changes from the liquid to the solid state is called its *freezing point*. (The term 'melting point' refers to the same temperature but applies to a change from solid to liquid.) The temperature at which a substance changes from the liquid to the vapour state is called its *boiling point*; an alternative term, used in property tables, is *saturation temperature*. It should be pointed out that both freezing and boiling points depend on pressure. The boiling point of water, for example, is 100 °C at standard atmospheric pressure but will be higher for pressures above atmospheric: in a pressure cooker, for example, water boils at about 120 °C. For pressures below atmospheric, the boiling point is below 100 °C and, using a vacuum pump, it may readily be demonstrated that if the pressure is sufficiently low, water will boil at room temperature. Pressure also has an effect on the freezing point of water, although the change produced is relatively small. Increasing the pressure lowers the freezing point so that in making a snowball, compressing a handful of ice crystals lowers their freezing point so that some melting occurs; on releasing the pressure the liquid thus formed re-freezes, binding the crystals together.

The heat transfer required to cause a change of state is called 'latent heat': the word 'latent' means 'hidden' and its use derives from the fact that no temperature change is observed. (Heat transfer not involving a change of state is sometimes called 'sensible heat' since it produces a change in temperature which can be 'sensed'.) Thus the *specific latent heat of fusion* is the amount of heat transfer required to change 1 kg of a substance from the solid to the liquid state at constant temperature and pressure, and the *specific latent heat of vaporization* is the amount of heat transfer required to change 1 kg of a substance from the liquid to the vapour state at constant temperature and pressure. The symbol L is used for specific latent heat, so that in both cases

$$Q = mL \qquad (10.4)$$

It should be noted that the change of state may be in either direction; both will involve the same amount of energy. Thus, the specific latent heat of fusion of ice is 335 kJ/kg, so that if 1 kg of ice at 0 °C is to be melted to produce 1 kg of water at 0 °C, 335 kJ of heat energy must be transferred to it: it would be equally true to say that there must be a heat transfer of 335 kJ *from* 1 kg of water at 0 °C in order to convert it into ice at 0 °C. Similarly, to evaporate 1 kg of water at atmospheric pressure and 100 °C, producing 1 kg of steam at 100 °C, requires a heat transfer of 2256.7 kJ: when 1 kg of steam at 100 °C condenses at constant pressure to form 1 kg of water at 100 °C, 2256.7 kJ of heat energy is given out.

The energy transfer involved during a change of state (i.e., the 'latent heat') must not be confused with the energy *contained* by the substance concerned. It might appear that the energy transferred is simply stored by the substance, to be given out again when the change is reversed but, particularly in the case of a liquid–vapour change, this is not quite true: two kinds of energy are involved. When water changes to steam, for example, two things happen: the molecular structure is altered, involving a change in the internal energy, but also the volume is greatly increased and, during this expansion, work will be done against the surrounding pressure; it may be shown that the work done in this way is equal to the product of the pressure and the change in volume. These two kinds of energy are combined in a property called *enthalpy* (H) which is measured in joules and is defined as the sum of internal energy and the product (pressure × volume):

$$H = U + pV \tag{10.5}$$

Thus, provided the pressure remains constant, the heat energy transferred to a substance is equal to the increase in its enthalpy, or

$$Q = H_2 - H_1 \tag{10.6}$$

The quantity listed in property tables is *specific enthalpy* (h) which is the enthalpy per kilogramme of substance. Thus for a change involving m kilogramme,

$$Q = m(h_2 - h_1) \tag{10.7}$$

Figure 10.1 is a graph showing how the enthalpy of 1 kg of water (i.e., its specific enthalpy) varies with temperature as the water is heated at constant pressure. At point A the water is at $0\,°C$ and, for practical purposes, its enthalpy may be taken as zero. Between A

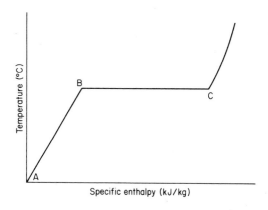

Figure 10.1

and B, heat is being supplied so that both enthalpy and temperature increase steadily until, at B, boiling point (or saturation temperature) is reached. During this period the water would be referred to as a *compressed liquid* or a *subcooled liquid* and at B (i.e., when the water is at its saturation temperature) it would be called a *saturated liquid*. After point B is reached, the water commences to boil, i.e., to change its state from liquid to vapour. Temperature remains constant but heat is being supplied and enthalpy increases until at C all the liquid has become vapour and this is called a *saturated vapour* (often, in this case, referred to as 'dry saturated steam' to emphasize the fact that it contains no liquid). From C onwards, further heat supply causes the temperature of the vapour to rise above saturation temperature and it is now called a *superheated vapour*.

10.5 Thermodynamic property tables

Property tables list the thermodynamic properties of fluids (that is, saturation temperature, specific enthalpy, and other properties) for a range of pressures; they are concerned mainly with the properties of water and steam, but often contain information about other fluids, particularly those used in refrigeration plants. For a given pressure, the section of the tables relating to 'saturated water and steam' will give firstly the saturation temperature t_s. For example, for a pressure of 5 bar, $t_s = 151.8\,°C$ and this means that at a pressure of 5 bar, water boils at 151.8 °C. (It should be noted that the pressures referred to in property tables are 'absolute pressures'; pressure gauges normally read pressure above atmospheric, and absolute pressure = gauge pressure + atmospheric pressure.) Another column of the table gives values of h_f, the specific enthalpy of saturated liquid (corresponding to point B in Fig. 10.1) and a further one gives values of h_g, the specific enthalpy of saturated vapour (corresponding to point C in Fig. 10.1): both are stated in kJ/kg. The difference between h_f and h_g is listed as h_{fg}, and it follows from Eq. 10.7 that this is the heat transfer required to convert 1 kg of saturated liquid to saturated vapour at constant pressure. This corresponds to the definition of the specific latent heat of vaporization, L, thus,

$$L = h_g - h_f = h_{fg} \qquad (10.8)$$

The tables also list other properties – specific volume v, specific internal energy u, and specific entropy s – which do not concern us at this stage. They do not, however, give the specific enthalpies of compressed or subcooled liquids (i.e., those corresponding to points between A and B in Fig. 10.1). However, for practical purposes, these may be found with sufficient accuracy by considering the specific enthalpy of water at $0\,°C$ as zero and by making use of Eqs 10.3 and 10.7:

$$Q = mct \quad \text{and} \quad Q = m(h_2 - h_1)$$

If we consider the heating of 1 kg of water at constant pressure from $0\,°C$ to the required temperature t, this gives (taking the specific heat capacity of water as $4180\ \text{J/kg}\,°C$):

$$Q = 1 \times 4180 \times t = 1(h - 0)$$
$$4180t = h \tag{10.9}$$

In other words, the specific enthalpy of compressed or subcooled water at a temperature $t\,°C$ is approximately equal to $4180\ t$ joules or $4.18\ t$ kilojoules.

The properties of superheated steam are found in another section of the tables and it will be seen that, for each pressure listed, values of specific enthalpy h (in kJ/kg) at various temperatures are given.

Worked examples

1. A copper pipe is 15 m long when installed at a temperature of $15\,°C$. By how much will its length increase when conveying hot water at $85\,°C$? The coefficient of linear expansion of copper is 17×10^{-6} per $°C$.

From Eq. 10.1,

$$\text{expansion } x = \alpha l t$$

Here the temperature rise $t = (85 - 15) = 70\,°C$
hence,

$$x = 17 \times 10^{-6} \times 15 \times 70$$
$$= 17.85 \times 10^{-3} \text{ m or } 17.85 \text{ mm}$$

2. A steel gauge block has a length of 100 mm at the standard temperature of $20\,°C$. If the coefficient of linear expansion of steel is 12×10^{-6} per $°C$ what will be its length at (a) $25\,°C$, (b) $10\,°C$?

(a) From Eq. 10.1,

$$\text{expansion } x = \alpha l t$$

Here the temperature rise $t = (25 - 20) = 5\,°C$
hence,

$$x = 12 \times 10^{-6} \times 100 \times 5$$
$$= 6 \times 10^{-3} \text{ or } 0.006 \text{ mm}$$
$$\text{length at } 25\,°C = 100 + 0.006$$
$$= 100.006 \text{ mm}$$

(b) From Eq. 10.1,

$$x = \alpha l t$$

In this case, x represents the *contraction* for a *fall* in temperature t and $t = (20 - 10) = 10\,°C$.

$$\text{hence, contraction } x = 12 \times 10^{-6} \times 100 \times 10$$
$$= 12 \times 10^{-3} \text{ or } 0.012 \text{ mm}$$
$$\text{length at } 10\,°C = 100 - 0.012$$
$$= 99.988 \text{ mm}$$

3. The starter ring for a petrol engine is to be fitted to the flywheel by 'shrinking on'. If, at $15\,°C$, the flywheel diameter is 500 mm and the internal diameter of the ring is 499.75 mm, to what temperature must the ring be heated if it is to be fitted over the flywheel with a clearance of 0.1 mm? The coefficient of linear expansion is 12×10^{-6} per $°C$.

$$\text{Required increase in diameter of ring} = 500 + 0.1 - 499.75$$
$$= 0.35 \text{ mm}$$

From Eq. 10.1,

$$x = \alpha l t$$

hence

$$0.35 = 12 \times 10^{-6} \times 499.75 \times t$$

Required temperature rise

$$t = \frac{0.35}{12 \times 10^{-6} \times 499.75}$$
$$= 58.36\,°C$$

Initial temperature $= 15\,°C$, hence the required final temperature is $(58.36 + 15) = 73.36\,°C$.

4. The bulb of a mercury-in-steel thermometer contains 5 ml of mercury at $20\,°C$. What will be the volume of the mercury at (a) $170\,°C$, (b) $-30\,°C$, if the coefficient of volumetric expansion of mercury is 180×10^{-6} per $°C$?

(a) From Eq. 10.2,

$$\text{increase in volume } v = \gamma V t$$

Here temperature rise

$$t = (170 - 20) = 150\,°C$$

hence

$$v = 180 \times 10^{-6} \times 5 \times 150$$
$$= 13.5 \times 10^{-3} \text{ or } 0.135 \text{ ml}$$

Final volume of mercury $= 5 + 0.135$
$$= 5.135 \text{ ml}$$

(b) From Eq. 10.2,

$$v = \gamma V t$$

Here fall in temperature

$$t = 20 - (-30)$$
$$= 50 \,°C$$

hence,

$$decrease \text{ in volume } v = 180 \times 10^{-6} \times 5 \times 50$$
$$= 4.5 \times 10^{-3} \text{ or } 0.045 \text{ ml}$$

Final volume of mercury $= 5 - 0.045$
$$= 4.955 \text{ ml}$$

5. Alcohol has a density of 792 kg/m³ at 0° C and its coefficient of volumetric expansion is 0.0011 per °C. What will be its density at 50 °C?

1 m³ of alcohol at 0 °C has a mass of 792 kg. If the temperature is raised by 50 °C, the mass will be unchanged but the volume will increase by:

$$v = \gamma V t$$
$$= 0.0011 \times 1 \times 50$$
$$= 0.055 \text{ m}^3$$

Hence, volume at 50 °C is $(1 + 0.055) = 1.055$ m³

$$\text{Density} = \frac{\text{mass}}{\text{volume}}$$
$$= \frac{792}{1.055} = 750.7 \text{ kg/m}^3$$

6. What quantity of heat energy must be transferred to an aluminium casting of mass 5 kg in order to raise its temperature from 20 °C to 140 °C? The specific heat capacity of aluminium is 920 J/kg °C.

From Eq. 10.3,

$$Q = mct$$

and here temperature change
$$t = (140 - 20) = 120\,°C$$

hence, heat transfer
$$Q = 5 \times 920 \times 120$$
$$= 552\,000\,J \text{ or } 552\,kJ$$

7. An electric kettle made of copper has a mass of 0.6 kg and contains 1.5 kg of water. What heat transfer is required to raise the temperature from 20 °C to 100 °C, and how long will this take (assuming no heat loss) if the element is rated at 2 kW? The specific heat capacity of copper is 385 J/kg °C and that of water 4180 J/kg °C.

From Eq. 10.3,
$$Q = mct$$

and for both copper and water,
$$t = (100 - 20) = 80\,°C$$

hence for the copper,
$$Q = 0.6 \times 385 \times 80$$
$$= 18\,480\,J$$

and for the water,
$$Q = 1.5 \times 4180 \times 80$$
$$= 501\,600\,J$$

Total heat transfer required $= 18\,480 + 501\,600$
$$= 520\,080\,J \text{ or } 520.08\,kJ$$

Rate of energy transfer from element $= 2 \times 10^3\,W$ or $2 \times 10^3\,J/s$

hence time required is

$$\frac{520\,080}{2 \times 10^3} = 260.04\,s \text{ or } 4\,min\,20.04\,s$$

8. Steel components of total mass 2 kg at a temperature of 600 °C are dropped into a tank containing 10 kg water at 15 °C. Neglecting the heat capacity of the tank and assuming no heat losses, calculate the final temperature of the water. The specific heat capacity of steel is 480 J/kg °C and that of water 4180 J/kg °C.

Heat transferred from steel = heat transferred to water

Let the final temperature of the water (and of the steel components) be t_F °C.

From Eq. 10.3,

$$\text{heat transfer } Q = mct$$

For steel, temperature change is from 600 °C to t_F °C, hence heat transferred from steel is $2 \times 480 \times (600 - t_F)$. For water, temperature change is from 15 °C to t_F °C, hence heat transferred to water is $10 \times 4180 \times (t_F - 15)$.

Equating heat transfers:

$$2 \times 480 \times (600 - t_F) = 10 \times 4180 \times (t_F - 15)$$
$$576\,000 - 960\,t_F = 41\,800\,t_F - 627\,000$$
$$1\,203\,000 = 42\,760\,t_F$$
$$t_F = \frac{1\,203\,000}{42\,760} = 28.13\,°C$$

9. A mass of 5 kg of aluminium at 20 °C is to be raised to its melting point of 660 °C and then melted completely. Calculate the amount of heat energy required. The specific heat capacity of aluminium is 920 J/kg °C and its specific latent heat of fusion is 400 kJ/kg.

Heat transfer required to raise temperature to melting point:
From Eq. 10.3,

$$Q = mct$$
$$= 5 \times 920 \times (660 - 20)$$
$$= 2.944 \times 10^6 \text{ J or } 2.944 \text{ MJ}$$

Heat transfer required to melt the metal:
From Eq. 10.4,

$$Q = mL$$
$$= 5 \times 400 \times 10^3$$
$$= 2 \times 10^6 \text{ J or } 2 \text{ MJ}$$

Total heat energy required $= 2.944 \times 10^6 + 2 \times 10^6$

$$= 4.944 \times 10^6 \text{ J or } 4.944 \text{ MJ}$$

10. A block of ice of mass 1.5 kg at 0 °C is dropped into 10 kg of water at 50 °C. Assuming no heat loss, what will be the final temperature of the water? The specific heat capacity of water is 4180 J/kg °C and the specific latent heat of fusion of ice is 335 kJ/kg.

Heat transferred from water = heat transferred to ice
Let the final temperature be t_F °C.
For the water,

$$Q = mct$$

and

$$t = (50 - t_F)$$

hence

$$Q = 10 \times 4180 \times (50 - t_F)$$

The ice must first be melted, producing water at 0 °C, and the temperature of this water must then be raised to the final temperature t_F.
Hence for the ice,

$$Q = mL + mct$$

and here

$$t = (t_F - 0)$$

hence,

$$Q = 1.5 \times 335 \times 10^3 + 1.5 \times 4180 \times (t_F - 0)$$

Equating the heat transfers,

$$10 \times 4180 \times (50 - t_F) = 1.5 \times 335 \times 10^3 + 1.5 \times 4180 \times (t_F - 0)$$

$$2090 \times 10^3 - 41\,800\, t_F = 502.5 \times 10^3 + 6270\, t_F$$

$$1587.5 \times 10^3 = 48\,070\, t_F$$

$$t_F = \frac{1587.5 \times 10^3}{48\,070} = 33.02\ °C$$

11. A vessel contains 2 kg of water at 15 °C and atmospheric pressure. What quantity of heat energy must be transferred to this water to convert it completely into steam at 100 °C? The specific heat capacity of water is 4180 J/kg °C and its specific latent heat of vaporization is 2256.7 kJ/kg.

The temperature of the water must first be raised to 100 °C, then it must be converted into steam.

$$Q = mct + mL$$

and here

$$t = (100 - 15) = 85\ °C$$

hence

$$Q = 2 \times 4180 \times 85 + 2 \times 2256.7 \times 10^3$$
$$= 710.6 \times 10^3 + 4513.4 \times 10^3$$
$$= 5224 \times 10^3 \text{ J or } 5224 \text{ kJ}$$

12. Using property tables, state: (a) the boiling point of water when at an absolute pressure of 10 bar; (b) the specific enthalpy of saturated steam at this pressure; (c) the specific latent heat of vaporization of water for this pressure; and (d) the specific enthalpy of superheated steam at 10 bar and 300 °C.

(a) The 'boiling point' is referred to in the tables as the saturation temperature t_s. For a pressure $p = 10$ bar, $t_s = 179.9$ °C
(b) Specific enthalpy of saturated steam is found under the symbol h_g. For $p = 10$ bar, $h_g = 2778$ kJ/kg
(c) From Eq. 10.8,

$$L = h_g - h_f = h_{fg}$$
For $p = 10$ bar, $h_{fg} = 2015$ kJ/kg

(d) For $p = 10$ bar and $t = 300$ °C, the section of the tables dealing with superheated steam gives specific enthalpy $h = 3052$ kJ/kg.

13. Water enters a boiler at 20 °C. The boiler pressure is 15 bar and steam leaves its superheater at 350 °C. What quantity of heat energy must be transferred to the boiler for every 5 kg of water evaporated?

From Eq. 10.7,

$$Q = m(h_2 - h_1)$$

For the water entering the boiler, from Eq. 10.9,

$$h = 4180 t$$

hence,

$$h_1 = 4180 \times 20 = 83\,600 \text{ J/kg or } 83.6 \text{ kJ/kg}$$

For the steam leaving the boiler, property tables give (for $p = 15$ bar and $t = 350$ °C),

$$h_2 = 3148 \text{ kJ/kg}$$

Hence, for every 5 kg of water evaporated,

$$Q = 5 \times (3148 - 83.6)$$
$$= 15\,322 \text{ kJ or } 15.322 \text{ MJ}$$

Problems

1. A steel bridge is 50 m long at 15 °C. By how much will its length alter: (a) when its temperature rises to 25 °C; (b) when its temperature falls to −5 °C? The coefficient of linear expansion of steel is 12×10^{-6} per °C.

(*Answer.* (a) 6 mm expansion (b) 12 mm contraction.)

2. A brass bar has a length of 800 mm at 20 °C. When heated to 100 °C its length is found to increase by 1.25 mm. What is the coefficient of linear expansion of brass?

(*Answer.* 19.53×10^{-6} per °C.)

3. An aluminium casting is 250 mm long at the moment the molten metal solidifies at 660 °C. If the coefficient of linear expansion of aluminium is 24×10^{-6} per °C, what will be the length of the casting when it has cooled down to 15 °C?

(*Answer.* 246.13 mm.)

4. A precision steel length bar has a length of 500 mm and is calibrated at 20 °C. What will be its length at (a) 26 °C, (b) 12 °C? The coefficient of linear expansion of steel is 12×10^{-6} per °C.

(*Answer.* (a) 500.036 mm (b) 499.952 mm.)

5. A collar of 149.85 mm bore is to be 'shrunk' on to a shaft of diameter 150 mm (both dimensions being measured at 20 °C). To what temperature must the collar be heated before it can be fitted over the shaft with a diametral clearance of 0.1 mm? The coefficient of linear expansion is 12×10^{-6} per °C.

(*Answer.* 159 °C.)

6. A bronze bush is to be an interference fit in a bore and is to be fitted by cooling it using solid carbon dioxide. If, at 20 °C, the outside diameter of the bush is 50.05 mm and the bore diameter is 50 mm, to what must the temperature of the bush be reduced before it can be fitted in with a diametral clearance of 0.01 mm? The coefficient of linear expansion of the bronze is 17×10^{-6} per °C.

(*Answer.* −50.5 °C.)

7. A steel shaft of diameter 80 mm runs in a brass bearing and, with both components at 15 °C, there is a diametral clearance of 0.06 mm. If the coefficient of linear expansion of steel is 12×10^{-6} per °C and that of brass 19×10^{-6} per °C, what will the diametral clearance become when both shaft and bearing are at 60 °C?

(*Answer.* 0.0852 mm.)

8. The diameter of an aluminium component is measured using a steel micrometer. The temperature of both is 10 °C and the micrometer reading is 41.67 mm. What reading would have been obtained if the temperature of both component and micrometer had been 20 °C? The coefficient of linear expansion of aluminium is 24×10^{-6} per °C and that of steel 12×10^{-6} per °C.

(*Answer.* 41.675 mm.)

9. A tank contains 400 m³ of water at 10 °C. If the coefficient of volumetric expansion of water is 150×10^{-6} per °C, by how much will the volume of the water increase when its temperature is raised to 25 °C?

(*Answer.* 0.9 m³.)

10. A thermometer bulb contains 2.5 ml of alchohol at 15 °C. What will be the volume of the alcohol at (a) 65 °C, (b) −25 °C? The coefficient of volumetric expansion of alcohol is 0.0011 per °C.

(*Answer.* (a) 2.6375 ml (b) 2.39 ml.)

11. A certain oil has a density of 920 kg/m³ at 0 °C and its coefficient of volumetric expansion is 700×10^{-6} per °C. What will be its density at 100 °C?

(*Answer.* 859.8 kg/m³.)

12. The density of mercury at 20 °C is 13 547 kg/m³. If the coefficient of volumetric expansion of mercury is 180×10^{-6} per °C, what will be its density at −30 °C?

(*Answer.* 13 670 kg/m³.)

13. What quantity of heat energy must be transferred in order to raise the temperature of a steel component of mass 5 kg from 20 °C to 600 °C? The specific heat capacity of steel is 480 J/kg °C.

(*Answer.* 1.392 MJ.)

14. An iron casting of mass 2 kg cools down from 1000 °C to 25 °C. If the specific heat capacity of cast iron is 500 J/kg °C, what will be the heat transfer from the casting to its surroundings?

(*Answer.* 975 kJ.)

15. The sole plate of an electric iron is made of aluminium and has a mass of 0.6 kg. What quantity of heat energy must be transferred to the plate if its temperature is to be raised from 20 °C to 170 °C, and how long will this take (assuming no heat loss) if its

heating element is rated at 800 W? The specific heat capacity of aluminium is 920 J/kg °C.

(*Answer.* 82.8 kJ, 1 min 43.5 s.)

16. An electric kettle made of copper has a mass of 0.8 kg and contains 1 kg of water at 10 °C. What heat transfer is required if the temperature is to be raised to 100 °C and, assuming no heat loss, how long will this take if the kettle has a 2 kW element? The specific heat capacity of copper is 385 J/kg °C and that of water 4180 J/kg °C.

(*Answer.* 403.92 kJ, 3 min 21.96 s.)

17. A domestic hot-water tank contains 75 kg of water at 15 °C. A 4 kW immersion heater is switched on. Neglecting the heat capacity of the tank and assuming no heat loss, what will be the water temperature after 1 hour? The specific heat capacity of water is 4180 J/kg °C.

(*Answer.* 60.93 °C.)

18. Steel components of total mass 3 kg at a temperature of 700 °C are quenched by dropping them into a tank containing 20 kg of oil at 20 °C. Taking the specific heat capacity of the oil as 2500 J/kg °C and that of steel as 480 J/kg °C, neglecting the heat capacity of the tank and assuming no heat loss, calculate the final temperature of the oil.

(*Answer.* 39.04 °C.)

19. A block of metal of mass 1.6 kg is placed in water boiling at 100 °C and allowed to remain there until it is at this temperature. It is then quickly transferred to a copper calorimeter (insulated to prevent heat loss) of mass 0.2 kg containing 2 kg of water at 10 °C. A thermometer shows that the water temperature rises to 19.5 °C. Taking the specific heat capacity of copper as 385 J/kg °C and that of water as 4180 J/kg °C, calculate the specific heat capacity of the metal.

(*Answer.* 622.3 J/kg °C.)

20. What quantity of heat energy must be transferred to 15 kg of ice at 0 °C to melt it completely, producing 15 kg of water at 0 °C? The specific latent heat of fusion of ice is 335 kJ/kg.

(*Answer.* 5.025 MJ.)

21. What quantity of heat energy must be transferred to 8 kg of copper at 20 °C to raise it to its melting point of 1083 °C and melt it

completely? The specific heat capacity of copper is 385 J/kg °C and its specific latent heat of fusion is 200 kJ/kg.

(*Answer.* 4.874 MJ.)

22. What quantity of heat energy must be extracted from 2 kg of water at 25 °C in order to convert it into ice at 0 °C? The specific heat capacity of water is 4180 J/kg °C and the specific latent heat of fusion of ice is 335 kJ/kg.

(*Answer.* 879 kJ.)

23. A quantity of ice of mass 0.5 kg at 0 °C is dropped into 4 kg of water at 40 °C. Assuming no heat loss, what will be the final temperature of the water? The specific heat capacity of water is 4180 J/kg °C and the specific latent heat of fusion of ice is 335 kJ/kg.

(*Answer.* 26.65 °C.)

24. What quantity of heat energy must be transferred to 0.5 kg of water at 25 °C and atmospheric pressure in order to convert it completely to steam at 100 °C? The specific heat capacity of water is 4180 J/kg °C and its specific latent heat of vaporization is 2256.7 kJ/kg.

(*Answer.* 1285.1 kJ.)

25. An electric kettle contains water boiling at atmospheric pressure and 100 °C. If its element is rated at 2 kW, how much water will be converted to steam in 1 minute? The specific latent heat of vaporization of water is 2256.7 kJ/kg.

(*Answer.* 0.0532 kg.)

26. 0.4 kg of steam at atmospheric pressure and 100 °C is passed into a tank containing 5 kg of water at 10 °C. Neglecting the heat capacity of the tank and assuming no heat loss, calculate the final temperature of the water. The specific heat capacity of water is 4180 J/kg °C and its specific latent heat of vaporization is 2256.7 kJ/kg.

(*Answer.* 56.66 °C.)

27. Using property tables, state: (a) the temperature at which water at an absolute pressure of 15 bar would change its state from liquid to vapour; (b) the specific enthalpy of water at this pressure and temperature; and (c) the specific enthalpy of saturated steam at this pressure.

(*Answer.* (a) 198.3 °C (b) 845 kJ/kg (c) 2792 kJ/kg.)

28. Use property tables to find: (a) the boiling point of water when at an absolute pressure of 2 bar; (b) the specific latent heat of vaporization of water at this pressure.

(*Answer.* (a) 120.2 °C (b) 220 kJ/kg.)

29. Use property tables to find the specific enthalpy of: (a) steam at an absolute pressure of 3 bar and temperature 200 °C; (b) steam at an absolute pressure of 30 bar and temperature 500 °C.

(*Answer.* (a) 2866 kJ/kg (b) 3456 kJ/kg.)

30. What quantity of heat energy must be transferred to 10 kg of water at an absolute pressure of 20 bar and temperature 30 °C in order to convert it, at constant pressure, to saturated steam?

(*Answer.* 26 736 kJ.)

Index